W9-DJN-650

The Rossetti-Leyland Letters

Frederick Richard Leyland

oval crayon drawing by Dante Gabriel Rossetti (1879)

THE ROSSETTI-LEYLAND LETTERS:

*The Correspondence of
an Artist and his Patron*

EDITED BY

Francis L. Fennell Jr.

Ohio University Press
Athens, Ohio

Introduction and Notes Copyright © 1978 by Francis L. Fennell, Jr.
Rossetti Letters Copyright © 1978 by William E. Fredeman and Imogen Dennis
Leyland Letters Copyright © 1978 by Ohio University Press
ISBN 0-8214-0207-2
Library of Congress Catalog Number 75-14552
Printed in the United States by
Oberlin Printing Company, Inc.

To my Parents
with great affection

Contents

42297

Dante Gabriel Rossetti (1870's)

Introduction

> The relations of Dante Gabriel Rossetti with his picture buyers
> . . . would offer an interesting study, and one that might serve
> to correct some misapprehensions. There is a very human side
> to these relations, much fun and friendly give and take, not a
> little procrastination and confusion, some irritation on both
> sides, and withal, so anachronistic a chronology and so
> intricate an accountancy that a chartered accountant would
> be needed to collaborate.[1]

The study which Helen Rossetti Angeli called for twenty—
five years ago has not been possible before. Five defective
copies of letters to Frederick Leyland, Rossetti's most important patron, and a scattering of letters to other buyers are
all that can be found in the Doughty—Wahl edition of Rossetti's correspondence. But with the publication of this correspondence between Rossetti and his chief patron, material
for such a study is now at hand. The 137 new letters published
here, 103 from Rossetti to Leyland and thirty—four from
Leyland to Rossetti, document a business relationship that
extended over sixteen years and that involved enough in-
tricacy and confusion to satisfy the most ambitious accoun-
tant. They show us the human side too, the "fun and friendly
give and take," the ebb and flow of what became, in the

1. Helen Rossetti Angeli, *Dante Gabriel Rossetti: His Friends and Enemies* (London:
Hamilton, 1949), p. 25.

words of Leyland's son-in-law Val Prinsep, "the one real friendship in [Leyland's] life."

Rossetti and his associates fascinate us. In the past ten years there have been no less than fifteen books dealing with the Pre–Raphaelite movement,[2] more than in the entire preceding century. Four anthologies of Pre–Raphaelite literature have been published,[3] several early critical works have been reissued, and recent exhibitions of Pre–Raphaelite art have drawn an enthusiastic critical response. Rossetti, as the central figure among the Pre–Raphaelites, has been a natural beneficiary of this renewed interest. In these same few years he has been the subject of six books of criticism[4] and dozens of scholarly articles. The publication of primary materials has also kept pace, the Doughty–Wahl edition of the correspondence and Virginia Surtees' splendid *catalogue raisonné* being the most important contributions.

This book makes a further contribution to the primary material on Rossetti. But it has another function as well. Like other more specialized collections, such as *The Letters of Dante Gabriel Rossetti to His Publisher F. S. Ellis,*[5] *The Rossetti-Macmillan*

2. G. H. Fleming, *Rossetti and the Pre–Raphaelite Brotherhood* (London, 1967) and *That Ne'er Shall Meet Again* (London, 1971); William Fredeman, ed. *The P. R. B. Journal* (Oxford, 1975); Martin Harrison, ed. *Pre–Raphaelite Paintings and Graphics* (New York, 1973); Timothy Hilton, *The Pre–Raphaelites* (New York, 1970); R. S. Hosman, *The Germ: A Pre–Raphaelite Little Magazine* (Miami, 1970); J. D. Hunt, *The Pre–Raphaelite Imagination 1848-1900* (London, 1968); David Larkin, ed. *The English Dreamers: A Collection of Pre–Raphaelite Paintings* (New York, 1975); John Nicoll, *The Pre–Raphaelites* (London, 1970); Graham Ovenden, *Pre–Raphaelite Photography* (London, 1972); James Sambrook, ed. *Pre–Raphaelitism: A Collection of Critical Essays* (Chicago, 1974); Allen Staley, *The Pre–Raphaelite Landscape* (Oxford, 1973); Lionel Stevenson, *The Pre–Raphaelite Poets* (Chapel Hill, N. C., 1972); Raymond Watkinson, *Pre–Raphaelite Art and Design* (London, 1970); Stanley Weintraub, *Four Rossettis: A Victorian Biography* (New York, 1976).

3. Jerome H. Buckley, ed. *The Pre–Raphaelites* (New York, 1968); C. Y. Lang, ed. *The Pre–Raphaelites and their Circle* (Boston, 1968); James Merritt, ed. *The Pre–Raphaelite Poem* (New York, 1966); Derek Stanford, ed. *Pre–Raphaelite Writing: an Anthology* (Totowa, New Jersey, 1973).

4. Robert Cooper, *Lost on Both Sides* (Athens, Ohio, 1970); Ronnalie Howard, *The Dark Glass: Vision and Technique in the Poetry of Dante Gabriel Rossetti* (Athens, Ohio, 1972); Robert Johnston, *Dante Gabriel Rossetti* (New York, 1969); John Nicholls, *Rossetti* (London, 1976); David Sonstroem, *Rossetti and the Fair Lady* (Middletown, Conn., 1970); J. F. Vogel, *Dante Gabriel Rossetti's Versecraft* (Gainesville, Fla., 1971).

5. Ed. Oswald Doughty (London: Scholartis Press, 1928).

Letters,[6] *Three Rossettis,*[7] and *Dante Gabriel Rossetti and Jane Morris: Their Correspondence,*[8] it dramatizes a relationship which is of special importance to our understanding of Rossetti's life. Most areas of that life—his love affairs, his addiction to chloral, his psychoses—have been explored fully, perhaps too fully. But some other parts, especially his relations with his buyers, have been less understood, and it is here that this collection gives us new perspectives.

We know that for the greater part of his adult life Rossetti was dependent upon the earnings from his paintings to maintain himself and his household. Nor should we forget what a household it was: a salaried art assistant (Knewstub, later Dunn); Fanny Cornforth; delinquent tenants like John Cattermole and his family; cooks, maids, valets; a private secretary (George Hake); frequent visitors and guests; and presiding over all, Rossetti himself, with his sumptuous living style and his indulgences in blue china or wombats. The establishment at Cheyne Walk was costly enough, but in addition for several years he had a joint tenancy of Kelmscott Manor, and he often maintained separate lodgings for Fanny. When we consider the expenses he must have incurred, we cannot wonder that Rossetti's need for "tin" was insatiable.

How could a man who never exhibited in public after the age of twenty–one, an artist whose work was cut off from the more usual avenues of attention and appreciation, still keep himself in such a grand fashion? Rossetti's remedy for this problem was to cultivate a select circle of wealthy patrons, men who could be counted on to vie with one another to possess whatever he painted. Their interest, their willingness to attract other buyers, and their jealousy over the quality of their own collections, enabled Rossetti to avoid public exhibition and rely instead on manipulating their responses to his work. Two in particular were especially valuable: Frederick R. Leyland, a Liverpool shipowner, and William Graham, an

6. Ed. Lona Mosk Packer (Berkeley, Cal.: University of California Press, 1963).
7. Ed. Janet Camp Troxell (Cambridge, Mass.: Harvard University Press, 1937).
8. Ed. John Bryson (Oxford, 1976).

M. P. from Glasgow. Exact figures cannot be determined, but by conservative estimate each paid Rossetti between £8,000 and £10,000 over the last sixteen years of his life. That amounts to an average of over £1,000 a year from them alone, a substantial sum a hundred years ago and income that Rossetti depended upon heavily.

A host of important questions arise. How did Rossetti secure these patrons in the first place? A more difficult feat, how did he persuade them to buy from him so frequently and over so long a period of time? How did friendship affect business, or business, friendship? Given Rossetti's constant need for money, we know he must have been guided by a desire to protect these sources of income, but in what way was he guided? A related and even more important issue, how was his art encouraged, or promoted, or distorted, or perhaps even destroyed by these same ties? The letters published here give us the material we need to begin answering these questions.

Among Rossetti's buyers, the most important was Frederick Richard Leyland (1831-1892). No patron spent more money on commissions than he, and none maintained his relationship with the artist over so long a time. Moreover Leyland was the kind of buyer who made demands on Rossetti's art, who helped determine the shape and direction of that art. And the rather surprising friendship which grew up between these men who were in so many ways dissimilar is itself an important dimension of Rossetti's life.

Thus Leyland becomes the focal point for an examination of Rossetti and his buyers. Any opportunity or any problem which characterizes the other relationships can be found here writ large. Similarly, whatever judgments we make about Rossetti and Leyland will have a wider application as well.

Frederick Leyland must have gladdened the heart of Samuel Smiles. Starting as an apprentice in the firm of Messrs. Bibby and Sons, Liverpool shipowners, Leyland was able to take over management of the company by the age of thirty. Within a few years he was able to buy out the surviving partners ("only not transporting them in the bargain," as Rossetti observed caustically) and to reorganize the company under his own name. His innovative designs for cargo vessels revolutionized British shipping. Later, seeking other worlds to conquer, he accepted the presidency of the fledgling National Telephone Company. When he died of a sudden heart attack in January of 1892, the "industrious apprentice" left an estate valued at £1 million.

It was Leyland's pleasure to spend a substantial portion of his immense wealth on the purchase of paintings, sculpture, and *objets d'art*. The sale of part of his collection at Christie's in May of 1892 brought in over £50,000. He also spent huge sums on the interior decoration of his homes. He bought the gilded grand staircase at Northumberland House and had it removed to his own town house at Prince's Gate. Whistler was commissioned to turn his dining hall into the famous Peacock Room. Morris and Company provided him with specially designed wallpaper and furniture. His collection of blue Nankin China rivaled Whistler's or Rossetti's.

In paintings Leyland bought a number of the old masters, such as Botticelli, Fra Filippo Lippi, Crivelli, Tintoretto, Giorgione, Velásquez, Rubens, Rembrandt, and Memling. But his real interest was in adorning his walls with the work of contemporary artists, and especially contemporary artists who were considered *avant–garde*, people who needed and would show their gratitude for his patronage. He bought from Whistler, Alphonse Legros, Frederic Leighton, and Albert Moore. His special affection was reserved for the Pre–Raphaelite school. He owned works by John Everett Millais, Ford Madox Brown, William Windus, James Smetham, Frederick Sandys, Edward Burne–Jones. And, pre–eminently, Rossetti.

Leyland first approached Rossetti in late December of 1865, at the recommendation of a Liverpool art dealer named John Miller. Miller was one of a number of provincial art dealers with whom Rossetti kept in contact and who, for a suitable commission, supplied him with new buyers. These new buyers were usually not Londoners; consequently, they were not tied so closely to the Royal Academy exhibitions and the other more common channels by which painters attracted attention. Furthermore their money tended to be "new" money, acquired through business rather than through birth, and they were perhaps willing to spend it in somewhat less conventional ways. Without dealers like Miller to recommend him, Rossetti would have been at a great financial disadvantage, and it is no accident that some of the best collections of Pre–Raphaelite art can still be found in provincial cities like Liverpool or Manchester.

Perhaps Leyland was also prompted by a chance connection, the fact that his daughters' governess, Louisa Parke, was an old friend of Rossetti's mother. We know that Louisa Parke was Mrs. Rossetti's house guest that same fall, and she may have brought back word of Rossetti's paintings and his enigmatic but attractive personality. In any event Leyland came to Rossetti's studio in late December, and he wanted very much to buy *Sibylla Palmifera*, which was then on the easel. Somehow the negotiations miscarried and the painting was promised to George Rae. The next work which Rossetti undertook, *Lady Lilith*, was a companion-piece to the *Palmifera*. Leyland eagerly accepted the opportunity to commission it. Within a year he had given Rossetti two other commissions. The total price stipulated by these agreements was in excess of £1,400.

During the course of these and later commissions Rossetti and Leyland became friends as well. "My dear Sir" in the letters becomes "My dear Rossetti" and then "My dear Gabriel." The two dined together often, either at Cheyne Walk or at Leyland's town residence. Leyland was a frequent visitor to Rossetti's studio, and he also journeyed to Kelmscott and later to Birchington–on–Sea. Rossetti in turn was offered the hospitality of Leyland's country estate, Speke Hall near Liverpool, although the artist was able to pay a lengthy visit only once, in August of 1868.

It was a friendship of remarkable contrasts. Leyland was stiff, reserved, excessively formal (he always wore frilled shirts, even in the daytime, long after they had gone out of style). His swift rise from apprentice to partner to sole owner showed a business acumen—and a ruthlessness—that might have qualified him as an example of Carlyle's self-made Captains of Industry. His family life was typical of the Victorian *nouveau riche,* son to Harrow and Cambridge, daughters marrying well, the close "family circle" dividing its time between London and the country. His letters show Leyland to have been exacting, methodical, and often quite peremptory in his demands ("Get Lucrezia off your hands. She can be doing no good in your dirty studio."). He is always direct, practical, avoiding social chitchat. We touch the inner emotions only once, in the short but poignant letter in which he announces the death of his eldest daughter.

Rossetti's private life on the other hand was, at least until his last years, expansive, bohemian, irreverent. He kept bachelor quarters and outrageous hours. The frequent presence of Fanny or Janey Morris, or the addiction to whiskey and chloral must have shocked the strait—laced Leyland. Rossetti borrowed and lent money with equal indifference, and when Leyland is exacting in these letters, Rossetti is casual and often careless. Leyland's directness contrasts with Rossetti's preference for circling around a point, for persuading by means of indirection and cajolery, for combining business with personal news and gossip.

But if there were differences, there were also some very real affinities. Both men shared a sense of being outsiders. Rossetti was of course marked off by his professions (painting and poetry), by his Italian ancestry, and by his unconventional living arrangements. Leyland suffered the fate of those who earned their money in trade rather than inheriting it. He was shut off from the "best circles," and when he died, the former apprentice, now one of the richest men in England, received only a miserably short, one—paragraph obituary notice in the august *Times.*

Moreover both men were, in their own ways, quite ambitious, and they were shrewd enough to see ways in which their friendship could be mutually advantageous. Rossetti's needs were more obvious and more easily satisfied. He had to have "tin," lots of it, to fund his customary extravagances. Beyond this he wanted recognition, if not from exhibitions and prizes, then at least from a circle of knowledgeable picture buyers. All the better if these buyers were steady, reliable customers, who would spare the artist the necessity of hawking his wares. Leyland was immensely useful on both counts.

Leyland's need was equally pressing, but more subtle, because it was psychological rather than economic. He seems to have wanted to be a great merchant prince, a kind of Victorian Cosimo de' Medici, lavishing his wealth on deserving artists. The parallel with the Medicis is more than superficial. It was not sufficient for Leyland to merely buy paintings, or even commission them. Rather he wanted to be a friend of the artist, to be his "patron" in the old Roman sense of protector, benefactor. Most of the artists he befriended were about his own age (Rossetti, for example, was three years his senior, Whistler three years his junior), and he was lavish in his gifts and offers of hospitality. For example, when Whistler undertook portraits of the Leyland family, he was invited to spend several weeks in residence at Speke Hall. Later on he was given sole possession of the house at Prince's Gate until the Peacock Room could be completed. We are reminded of Browning's Fra Lippo, "lodging with a friend / Three streets off— . . . / I' the house that caps the corner."

Thus Leyland involved himself as closely as he could in the creation of all the works he commissioned from Rossetti. He usually visited the studio in Chelsea whenever he came up to London, checking on the progress of works being done for him, interesting himself in whatever other works Rossetti had to show, perhaps coming for dinner or a late evening chat. His letters show how he placed concrete restrictions on each work he purchased. It should have only one figure in it, for example, or it should be the same size as a certain other picture, or it should fit a particular wall in a particular room. Rossetti's letters in turn show that he felt obligated to help Leyland plan the décor of his home. We find Rossetti giving advice on everything from the wallpaper, which he designed for Leyland through Morris and Company, to the proper hanging of paintings. He also counselled Leyland on the purchase or disposal of works by rival artists. ("I went to see Hunt's picture. If the dealers offer it you at a small profit on the cost price of 10,000£, I should say on the whole, Dont buy.")

Leyland was prepared to reward handsomely for this special relationship. His commissions were frequent and steady, insuring an average income of perhaps £500 a year for these works alone. Leyland rarely haggled about prices, paying what was asked if he wanted the painting, refusing it outright if he did not. When Rossetti needed advances or loans, and he often did, they were readily available.

Beyond the money paid on commissions, there was a profusion of personal gifts from Leyland—braces of pheasants, crates of oranges, choice Burgundy, tickets to the Royal Opera. He was also willing to do favors, such as providing a job for the cousin of Rossetti's friend and agent Charles Augustus Howell. Later we find Leyland agreeing to overstate the price he was paying for a painting to help Rossetti keep his market value high, or pretending ownership at sales to help Rossetti dispose of unwanted pictures. Leyland bought from Rossetti's friends, like Smetham, Brown, Sandys, and Burne—Jones, and introduced him to new patrons like William Graham.

Rossetti was of course grateful. His letters show his sense of indebtedness and his respect for Leyland: "I have had from you both friendship and appreciation; both are rare, and I should wish to show that I am not unmindful of them." No one was in a better position to know Rossetti's mature opinion of Leyland than Theodore Watts—Dunton, and in his novel *Aylwin*, Watts—Dunton has his Rossetti—*manqué* (the painter D'Arcy) describe the character Symonds, who was modeled on Leyland, as "a man of great taste, with a real love of art and music."[9] Similarly, William Michael Rossetti calls him "a man of judgment and refinement."[10] Leyland was one of the very few friends with whom Rossetti never broke faith. Perhaps the last letter Rossetti ever wrote was addressed to Leyland (see Appendix, Letter D), and Leyland was numbered among the handful of people who gathered for the funeral service at Birchington—on—Sea.

9. *Aylwin* (New York: Dodd, Mead, 1899), p. 208.

10. *Dante Gabriel Rossetti: His Family Letters, with a Memoir* (London: Ellis, 1895), II, 341.

Nevertheless, grateful as he was, Rossetti sometimes found Leyland's solicitude rather difficult to endure. Leyland could be generous, but he was also demanding. Rossetti did not vent his irritations to their source. However his letters to other friends show that he occasionally found Leyland irksome, perhaps even a bit of a bore. "[I]f you could come when Leyland comes," he wrote to Madox Brown, "it *would* be a boon. . . . a vis–à–vis with L. is a dreadful prospect."[11] During the course of his one major quarrel with Leyland in 1873, Rossetti's resentment found its angriest expression. "I have often said that to be an artist is just the same thing as to be a whore, as far as dependence on the whims and fancies of individuals is concerned," he wrote, again to Madox Brown. "The natural impulse is to say simply— Leyland be d----d!—and so no doubt the whore feels but too often inclined to say and cannot."[12]

In truth Rossetti was ambivalent about Leyland. On the one hand, he was genuinely fond of him and grateful for his continued patronage. On the other hand, he chafed under the bondage which that gratitude imposed. This trait, feeling obligated and at the same time resenting that feeling, was a constant in Rossetti's character as early as his relationship with Lizzie Siddal. Then too his vexation was spurred by the fact that he was almost always deeply in debt to Leyland. That indebtedness could not be shrugged off, because it was rooted in a power that both men understood very well, the power of money. During the last sixteen years of his life Rossetti was Leyland's debtor in the literal sense of that term. For months at a time Rossetti met his enormous living expenses with what was in effect borrowed money.

The origin of his indebtedness to Leyland lay in Rossetti's method of accepting commissions. His procedure, as he outlines it to Leyland in his first letter, was common at the time and seems simple enough: "The mode of payment (should you wish to have [*Lady Lilith*]) £150 down, 150 on my showing you the picture far advanced . . . and the remainder

11. Oswald Doughty and John Robert Wahl, eds. *Letters of Dante Gabriel Rossetti* (London: Clarendon Press, 1967), III, 1292.
12. *Ibid.*, 1175.

on completion." Occasionally it works that way. The money comes in as the painting progresses and both parties are satisfied.

But affairs rarely progress so smoothly, as these letters show. The first problem is Rossetti's dilatory habits as a painter. His imagination teems with ideas, projects, schemes, and he is often able to persuade Leyland to commission his latest enthusiasm. But then, after the initial excitement, comes the hard work of getting that idea onto canvas. Weeks become months, become years, become (in the case of *La Pia de' Tolomei*) over a decade. The money has been paid, in part or in whole, but somehow the painting does not get finished. Inquiries from Leyland elicit a guilt–tinged promise of new diligence, or perhaps a puffed–up report of progress. But the record from these letters is all too clear: *Lady Lilith*, commissioned in 1866, promised for "speedy completion," was completely paid for by August of that year but not finished until 1868 or 1869. *The Roman Widow*, begun for Leyland in the spring of 1873, promised for the fall, then the winter, then the spring, then "no human likelihood" of its failing to be done by June—was delivered some time the next fall. *A Sea-Spell*, described as "in a most forward state" when commissioned in the summer of 1875, was delivered first in 1877 and then (after further work) re-delivered in 1881. *Mnemosyne*, commissioned in 1877, was completed in 1881. *La Pia de' Tolomei*, the most extreme example, commissioned in 1868, was not finished until thirteen years later, in 1881.

There was another, more complicated problem. We can see in these letters how the flush of Rossetti's enthusiasm will often secure him a commission. But then as time passes his appetite for the task slackens, to be replaced by a newer idea. Then comes a delicate question: Would Leyland consent to transfer the money paid down on the older commission to the price of this latest proposal? Leyland's alternatives are equally unattractive. He can accept the proposal, so that Rossetti will continue to paint for him and so that he can see tangible results for money already spent. But a man who has been promised one thing, and then is told that he cannot have it but must have something else, is perhaps going to be resentful. The other choice is to refuse the proposal. But then Rossetti would begin to paint for someone else, and the down payment would float in some limbo, destined to be applied toward unspecified future commissions. Either choice is unpalatable, and there can be little wonder that Leyland occasionally shows himself irritated. (Of course he knew there was no chance to reclaim the money itself. It would have been spent long since.)

Furthermore, when the money did float free temporarily, it was apt to be forgotten, or misapplied, or misrepresented. Rossetti's letters frequently acknowledge confusion or error: "By the bye I may as well here formally notify the errour in my last account sent to you. In reality the sum of £150 there remaining 'unattached' should have been 350£." (Letter 41) "I am a little foggy as to our relations to [the *Hero*]." (Letter 105) "I find there was a flattering unction in my view of the balance on the *Salutation*." (Letter 133)

Misunderstanding was inevitable. It culminated in the one major quarrel between Rossetti and Leyland, which occurred during the fall of 1873 and is dramatized here in Letters 55–62. This disagreement is worth studying closely. It reveals a great deal about the character of each participant. When we see what each insists upon and what each is willing to concede, we gain a better understanding of the nature of their relationship. And the resolution of this controversy offers insights into the way economic necessity came to distort Rossetti's art, and the way that relationships with Leyland and others contributed to Rossetti's abrupt decline as an artist.

The origin of the quarrel goes back to the previous spring. Because of physical and mental ailments, including an attempted suicide, Rossetti had been unable to paint for quite some time. When he resumed work in April he was conscious of an enormous floating debt to Leyland, over £1,000. He began *La Ghirlandata*, intending it for Leyland but not consulting him about it, as had been his custom before. When the picture was nearly finished he abruptly offered it, sight unseen. The price asked was 800 guineas, less only £200 allowed toward previous advances, and this price was coupled with an audacious request for another £400 on account (Letter 51).

Leyland, hearing from Howell that the picture had three heads in it, demurred, saying he would not buy it without first coming to Kelmscott to see it, and that he was in no mood to pay out further advances (Letter 52). Rossetti, irked that he could not have the full price for the picture if he sold it to Leyland, ignored the letter and sold the painting to William Graham for the full 800 guineas. Rossetti's motives were not as innocent as the ones he later professed to Leyland. In June he boasted to Dunn that he sold the painting "over Leyland's head." To Fanny Cornforth he recounted gleefully that "Leyland was to have had it, but he wanted to see it first and put me out of temper, so I offered it to Graham. . . . Leyland is ready to bite his own head off with vexation. . . . It will teach [him] not to miss another chance."[13]

Leyland was stung by this treatment. He was a patient man, all things considered, but when no work was forthcoming by early fall he was angry. He had paid out £1,050 and had nothing to show for it for over a year and a half. In his letter of 8 October he tells Rossetti bluntly that "I feel more disappointed than I can express," and warns that "we had better be understood as to how the affair is to be arranged."

Rossetti's first reaction was to take offense. When dealing with buyers his temper was always explosive—witness the vituperation of his letters to John Heugh or Walter Dunlop during prior controversies.[14] His reply to Leyland denies the charge of neglect and makes a threat of his own. "If the scheme is now so entirely altered, this must of course render it much more difficult for me to restrict myself during any long time together to my work for you. . . ." The implication is clearly that Rossetti will take his own sweet time about paying back the money unless he can arrange it his own way.

But Leyland in his turn was equally adamant. He under-

---

13. *Ibid.,* 1186, 1189, 1192.
14. *Ibid.,* II (1965), 572, 578.

takes a point–by–point refutation of Rossetti's arguments (Letter 58). He wants new work soon. *His* implication is even clearer: whoever pays the piper calls the tune.

Rossetti's choice was painful. He could vent his anger and respond as he had done in the Heugh and Dunlop affairs. Certainly the temptation was strong ("The natural impulse is to say simply—Leyland be d----d!"). But the Heugh and Dunlop quarrels were different. He did not owe them money and was not likely to obtain any from them in the immediate future. In this instance, however, he has had the free use of a considerable sum of Leyland's money, and he was sensitive to the implied moral obligations. More importantly, could he afford to alienate so loyal a buyer and so influential a friend? How much pride was he willing to swallow to maintain the relationship?

Certainly the precedents for compromise on Rossetti's part were not very encouraging. Over the preceding years Rossetti had managed to bring a rancorous end to almost every important friendship in his life. Ruskin, Swinburne, Meredith, Browning, Hunt, Millais—Rossetti had quarreled with them all, and put them out of his life. And he was to continue to do so, with his factotum Dunn or with the Hakes. But in the present case, surprisingly, he at last consents to see it Leyland's way. "I judge we are now agreed that you take the Proserpine, Roman Widow, & La Pia (or substitute, as I may be able to decide) at 800 guineas each, & levy my debt to you in equal proportions on the three." (Letter 59)

The crisis was an important one. Leyland and Rossetti agreed to continue in the same way, money to be advanced on work in progress. But some of the old equality and easy familiarity seem to have been lost. Rossetti's letters thereafter show resignation, almost subservience. There is a poignance in his yearning for their old camaraderie: "I thought it possible that a flying visit to town might bring the aroma of your cigarette & your friendly greeting through my darkling studio doorway as of old." (Letter 112) In the beginning Rossetti had been the dominant figure, Leyland the eager suitor. After 1873 the balance tipped markedly in Leyland's direction. Rossetti seems to have decided that he could not face a future in which Leyland's economic support might be lacking.

Worse, there are hints that Rossetti began to shape his art with the "Leyland market" ever more closely in his mind. "Would it suit you," he writes at one point, "that . . . I should defray the rest [of my advance] by a separate work, —either a £280 picture, or else a portrait of yourself or some member of your family? I wd try & do my best for it in either case. . . ." (Letter 112) No proposals of his own, no pen–and–ink sketches trying to give shape to the fertile imagination, no vigor or excitement. Rossetti found it easier instead to paint whatever he thought would please Leyland. Of the twelve major oils which Rossetti completed between the fall of 1873 and his death, fully half of them were purchased by Leyland.

Everyone is agreed that the paintings of Rossetti's last years show a marked decline in artistic power. This decline has been attributed by some to emotional and physical illness, and by others to the need for making potboilers to keep up his income. These explanations are not satisfactory. Illness need not diminish a talent, as artists like Keats have often shown us, and Rossetti's poetic faculty remained relatively unimpaired during this period. Moreover he had always had to paint for a living; that kind of economic pressure was nothing new. And he himself recognized no decline in his art at all, as we shall see later. Rather, he thought he was advancing, as did his friends and critics.

One of the chief values of this collection of letters is the way it suggests another explanation for this decline, and that is the degree to which Rossetti had come to rely on a very small circle of patrons. Lionel Robinson termed Rossetti not unfairly "painter–in–ordinary to a limited few."[15] Rossetti had to please their tastes alone. If they were pleased, and paid, he was satisfied. If they felt themselves well recompensed by the kind of work he was turning out in these years, he had no economic motive to produce something different or better.

15. "The Private Art Collections of London. The Late Mr. Frederick Leyland's in Prince's Gate," Art Journal, 54 (1892), 138.

These letters suggest that Rossetti became a prisoner, albeit a willing prisoner, of his own business arrangements. He prided himself on his independence, the hallmark of which was his refusal to allow his pictures to be exhibited. This independence has been treated by friends and critics alike as if it were an unmixed blessing. But ironically this "freedom" resulted in ever tighter constraints, especially in the 1870's, because at a time when his reputation was at its highest—witness the public acclaim which greeted *Dante's Dream* when it was shown in Liverpool, or the £2,1000 he received for *Astarte Syriaca*—he was shut off from the lucrative sales which public exhibition might have brought. Such exhibition would have attracted new buyers, new demands, new criticism. Instead Rossetti chose to execute the endless variations on Janey Morris or Alexa Wilding which pleased Leyland and Graham so well. He reminds us of nothing so much as Browning's Pictor Ignotus:

> monotonous I paint
> These endless cloisters and eternal aisles
> With the same series, Virgin, Babe and Saint
> With the same cold calm beautiful regard,—

Rossetti's circle of patrons could have made up for its smallness by its catholicity of taste. Unfortunately such was not the case. Leyland had a special fondness for music and pressed Rossetti for paintings of women playing instruments or singing. Graham's preferences were similarly narrow. He disliked any pictures which smacked of "realism," thus encouraging the solipsistic tendencies which were increasingly coming to disfigure Rossetti's art. Lawrence Valpy was an insufferable prude, to the point of forcing Rossetti to paint out a bare shoulder. In short, Rossetti's reliance on this group of buyers encouraged him to be repetitious and unadventurous.

Leyland, as the chief buyer of the last decade of Rossetti's life, is an excellent example of this narrowness. From the evidence of his letters, we can only conclude that Leyland's principal interest was in the size of his pictures. The insistence on size is unremitting. Leyland postpones a decision on commissioning the proposed "Boat of Love" because "I wish to know more about the size and scale of heads in the picture as in the Michael Scott picture I went to the extreme of height and this is an important consideration. . . ." (Letter 32) He asks if the *Bower Meadow* could be "two or three inches larger each way," and then demonstrates how serious he is about the issue by rejecting the painting because "I found it too small. . . ." (Letters 34 and 38) Commissions are often made contingent on size: "don't let the height . . . exceed seven feet—a few inches less would be all the better" (Letter 38); "I am willing to take the Proserpine and the Roman Widow . . . assuming this latter is of the same size as the Veronica. . . ." (Letter 56); "The second picture you have to paint is one the size of Veronica or the Roman Widow and I should prefer a picture of this size rather than that of the Proserpine which I find a difficult size to hang advantageously." (Letter 75) No matter how good a picture is, Leyland will reject it if the size is not suitable, as in the cases of *Lucrezia Borgia* and "La Ricordanza." (Letters 54 and 103) Even so deservedly famous a picture as *La Pia de' Tolomei* is almost dismissed because it is oblong rather than upright (Letter 56).

Rossetti was fully conscious of the fact that there was a Leyland "type" to which his paintings should conform if they were to please. "I have somehow got through a new Leyland painting of the usual kind," he writes to Madox Brown upon completing *A Sea-Spell*.[16] Of course size was a factor in establishing the type, but there were other ingredients as well. At least seven of the major oils which were intended for Leyland portrayed a woman singing or playing a stringed instrument. These included *A Christmas Carol, Veronica Veronese, The Bower Meadow, La Ghirlandata, The Roman Widow, A Sea–Spell*, and *Desdemona's Death–Song*. Leyland was an accomplished musician (after all it was he who suggested to Whistler the use of musical analogies like "symphony" and "nocturne" for titles of pictures). Rossetti played to this aspect of Leyland's character.

Furthermore Rossetti was always very careful to point out

16. *Letters*, III, 1354.

to Leyland the color harmonies which he was trying to achieve. The paintings done for Leyland show a higher proportion of what we might call "monochromatic" works than is found among Rossetti's works as a whole. Perhaps this too was a natural consideration when dealing with a patron of Whistler's. And as a final consideration, Rossetti felt he had to be careful not to offend Leyland's rather delicate sensibilities, for example fearing that the subject of *The Roman Widow* "is too 'painful' for the nerves of the British purchaser."

For every artist there is a danger that, if he does not have to please many, he will not please long. Rossetti knew what it took to please Leyland and a few others. Such paintings were easily executed and demanded little from the artist either in imaginative power or technical skill. We need only compare these last paintings with an early work like *Ecce Ancilla Domini!* to see the difference, because in the paintings of Rossetti's youth we can sense that adventurousness, that impatience both with his own limitations and with received opinion, which characterizes a significant artist. Again Browning comes to mind: in Rossetti's early works his reach *does* exceed his grasp. By the 1870's this was no longer true. The letters in this collection, especially the ones discussed in the preceding paragraphs, suggest that while Rossetti's small circle of buyers was undoubtedly an economic comfort, it may also have been a serious artistic danger.

These letters also enable us to discard the myth of Rossetti's shrewdness as a man of business. This reputation, fostered by contemporaries like Dunn and Rossetti's brother William Michael, and promoted by later critics like Oswald Doughty, has slim foundation. It is based mostly on Rossetti's delight in occasional flim–flammery, as exemplified here by his request to have Leyland force up the price on the repossessed *Lucrezia Borgia* (Letter 79), or by his raising the price of *Ligea Siren* by fifty guineas after Leyland rejected it (Letter 49).

But if ever a man was penny wise and pound foolish it was Rossetti. For example, he rarely kept detailed notes or records of his agreements with patrons, relying instead on his self–proclaimed "good memory." If disputes arose later over these agreements, as they often did because of his dilatory habits as a painter, he was entirely at the mercy of their records rather than his, and he usually had to sacrifice his claim. The dispute with Leyland in the fall of 1873 is an excellent example. Rossetti relies on his own recollection of a verbal agreement supposedly reached during an evening's conversation at Queen's Gate two years earlier. Leyland on the other hand has the documents, letters in which advances are asked against specific pictures. In the absence of any written memorandum about the conversation, it is an unequal contest. There are several like instances, with Rossetti lamenting that he cannot remember what had been arranged, or that his notes have gotten confused. Leyland is always the one to set it straight, in a clear, businesslike way: "The price of the Pia was as I said 800 gnas" (Letter 58); "I make the balance of Roman Widow £188 [not £192]" (Letter 77); "I merely write to put on record that the commission for Astarte is a new one—and quite independent of the old" (Letter 106); "I have looked at my memorandum of the payments on account of 'Hero' and 'La Pia' and find they are as follows. . . ." (Letter 115) Finally Leyland is reduced to spelling out exactly how money is to be appropriated and then, as if catechizing a schoolboy, asking Rossetti to repeat back to him how the money will be placed (Letter 111).

In addition Rossetti hardly ever bargained successfully over price. On the one occasion when he tried, over the commission for La Pia and the replica of Sibylla Palmifera jointly, Leyland came out 100 guineas ahead. In fact Rossetti more often had occasion to bemoan the fact that he sold works for less than he could have received (Letters 31 and 88, for example). And when we add to all of these lapses the needless quarrels which Rossetti provoked with other buyers like Graham, Heugh, Dunlop, Mathews, and Valpy, we must conclude that the image of Rossetti as a resourceful hustler, always contriving bargains to his best advantage, is simply not borne out by the evidence.

The matter of Rossetti's prices shows this lack of acumen. From his letters to Leyland we must conclude that he based his price almost exclusively on four factors: medium, size, number of figures, and presence or absence of "the ideal."

Rossetti's application of these factors in so rigid a way almost tempts us to apply to him Hardy's description of Browning, that he sometimes displayed qualities worthy of a dissenting grocer.

Since most of Rossetti's works during this period were in oil, the first of these four factors is usually not a variable. But consider the matter of size. Of course Rossetti had to take into account Leyland's strict requirements in this area. But he seems to have added to them his own rather crude notion that a small alteration in the dimensions of a picture should result in a proportionate adjustment of the cost. He describes *Mnemosyne*, for example, as being "enlarged to an 800 guinea picture." When the completed *Monna Rosa* turns out to be slightly larger than *The Loving Cup*, Rossetti congratulates himself for not raising the price accordingly. It's almost as if you bought paintings like you bought wallpaper, by the yard.

Similarly with the number of figures: because *La Ghirlandata* will have three heads in it, Rossetti proposes that its price be 100 guineas higher. It isn't a matter of whether the three figures are done better than a single figure, or vice versa. Like a portrait photographer, one does not offer three poses for the same price as one.

The issue of "the ideal" is somewhat more complicated. Rossetti's clearest statement of the importance of this principle occurs in Letter 88: "Indeed the *Proserpine* should in reality have been more highly priced, . . . [because] between ideal subjects of that kind & all others there is a gulf fixed. . . ." In another letter he contrasts *The Roman Widow* unfavorably with *Proserpine* "because of its lacking the sublimity of type which appears in that." (Letter 82) That "the ideal" was a factor in establishing price is also apparent in Letter 89, where Rossetti advises Leyland that "[I could not] by any possibility paint so important an ideal subject [as *Venus Astarte*] . . . for less than the 2000 guineas. . . ."

What is not so clear is the exact meaning which Rossetti assigned to this term. Presumably it had something to do with what in his poetry he called "the soul's sphere of infinite images," works which he described in the story "Hand and

Soul" as [things] "not to be seen of men." More concretely, both Proserpine and Venus, the two subjects directly associated with this term, are goddesses from Greek and Roman myth rather than subjects drawn from literature.

Perhaps for Rossetti this origin in myth gave them a symbolic dimension because mythological figures can more easily become embodiments of timeless qualities and attitudes. For example, *Proserpine* was designed to suggest "the feeling of Memory which might indeed equally be given as a name to the picture" (Letter 55). It can therefore be distinguished from a work like *Lucrezia Borgia* which portrays an historical event, or a work like *The Bower Meadow* which illustrates a passage from Dante. But Rossetti was never explicit on this point, despite the obvious importance he attached to it.

If the letters to Leyland revise our estimate of Rossetti's shrewdness, it was still true that he had to attract his patron to whatever new work he wished to offer. Consequently the reader of these letters is treated to frequent descriptions of new paintings. These descriptions in turn help us to see what Rossetti was trying to achieve in his work. For instance this enticement to buy *Proserpine*:

> . . . Since making the design, I have added details which do not appear in it or in the former picture,—some ivy in the background, & an incense–burner on the foreground slab of grey marble. In *beauty*, the picture much exceeds the sketch. The conception of the figure is connected with the legend by which Proserpine (having fatally partaken of a pomegranate in Hades & so excluded herself from permanent return to earth which would otherwise have been granted her) was permitted to spend one half of the year in the upper light & the other half in the shades of her new kingdom. The background of the figure—half light half shade—can however be accounted for on natural grounds (as needed in painting) since the opening of a door or window in a dim place with clear light outside would of course produce such an effect. The whole tone of the picture is a graduation of greys—from the watery blue–grey of the dress to the dim hue of the marble, all aiding the "Tartarean grey" which must be the sentiment of the subject. Proserpine looks yearningly towards the momentary light which strikes into her shadowy palace; and the clinging ivy

which strays over the wall (in the picture) further suggests the feeling of Memory which indeed might equally be given as a name to the picture. It is a very favorite design of mine, and I have composed a Sonnet for it both in Italian & in English. The former appears on the cartellino in the upper corner of the picture, & the latter on the frame below. There is nothing dismal or gloomy in the colour & lighting of this picture,—a tendency to such defect in the first picture having been one of the reasons which determined me to repeat it. The whole is meant to have a luminous mystic warmth such as we find in moonlight effects, & I believe I have succeeded. (Letter 55)

Similarly helpful is this description of *The Roman Widow*:

This [picture] I have cartooned from nature and am now beginning to paint it. It is called *Dis Manibus,*—the dedicatory inscription to the Manes, the initials of which (D M) we find heading the epitaphs in Roman cinerary urns. In the picture, a lady sits in the "Columbarium" beside her husband's urn which stands in a niche in the wall, wreathed about with roses & having her silver marriage–girdle hanging among them. Her dress is white—the mourning of nobles in Rome— and as she sits she plays on two harps (one in her arm & one lying beside her) her elegy addressed "Dis Manibus." The white marble background & urn, the white drapery & white roses will combine I trust to a lovely effect, & the expression will I believe be as beautiful & elevated as any I have attempted. Do you like me to consider this picture as yours at 800 gs? (Letter 55)

The emphasis on color harmony, the musical instruments, the interaction of painting and poem, the melancholy subject and mood, the typically Pre–Raphaelite insistence on "natural-ness" in color and lighting: these and other characteristics of Rossetti's paintings are quite consciously articulated in the letters to Leyland.

Moreover we are constantly reminded of the difficulties which assailed Rossetti while completing a picture. Many of these difficulties stemmed from his methods of composition. Of particular importance was his typically Pre–Raphaelite de-termination to always paint "from nature." His letters apolo-gize for delays by complaining that a model has been ill, or a particular costume has not arrived, or a suitable cat has not been found. If Rossetti is to paint roses, they cannot be just any roses:

> [*The Roman Widow*] is so nearly done that it seems a pity now for you to see it till quite finished; & this consummation is unluckily delayed by the non–appearance as yet of suitable roses. My own garden here failing me, I sent to some rose growers at Reading, but the specimens they send from my description do not answer, & there is nothing for it but to wait. Moreover there are wild roses needed too, & these no rose grower could supply in any case except the grower of all roses whoever he may be. (Letter 78)

If *A Sea–Spell* is delayed, the cause is a negligent taxidermist:

> It is in a most forward state—indeed would doubtless be finished now if there had not been an endless delay in getting a sea–gull set up by a naturalist in the position in which I need to paint him. This bird I am now promised at last tomorrow, & besides this there are only very minor details to add. . . . (Letter 92)

Rossetti seems to have been almost completely helpless unless he could paint from a model. He always painted from nature rather than from memory or the imagination. If the "endless madonnas" completed during his last years seem to us particularly lurid, it was not because he was trying to paint from his mind's eye. Quite literally, he *saw* them that way.

Poignantly, what we view as decline, Rossetti saw as progress. The letters to Leyland are a continual reaffirmation of that belief:

> *Lady Lilith*—"will be of my best" (Letter 1)
> *Lucrezia Borgia*—"one of my very best things" (Letter 15)
> *Bocca Baciata*—"decidedly one of my best watercolours" (Letter 18)
> *The Bower Meadow*—"one of my best things" (Letter 30)
> *Veronica Veronese*—"much the best I have ever done" (Letter 37)
> *Proserpine*—"is my best" (Letter 66)
> *The Roman Widow*—"as good a thing as ever I did" (Letter 72)
> *La Bello Mano*—"the *very best of its kind* I have done" (Letter 85)
> *A Sea–Spell*—"as brilliant in painting as anything I have done" (Letter 89)
> *Mnemosyne*—"I feel sure I never did a better thing" (Letter 102)

These claims might be dismissed as merely enticements to buy were it not for the letters to other friends which echo them. Furthermore, as several letters in this collection demonstrate, Rossetti wherever possible took great pains to retouch older works of his which Leyland owned, in order to make them conform to his newer style. And he was supported in this belief in the superiority of his later work. We find Leyland complimenting Rossetti on "how much better your work is" and expressing his gratitude for the "immense improvement" which later alterations have made.

There is a sad irony here. Rossetti did not go blind, as he so often feared he would. But in his last years he could no longer "see."

Prefatory Notes

As far as possible, these letters are reproduced just as they were written, including spelling, punctuation, abbreviations, and especially format. Parentheses are the writer's own; brackets designate whatever editorial intrusions are necessary.

The letters from Rossetti can be found in the Manuscript Division of the Library of Congress. Readers who wish bibliographical descriptions or exact locations for these letters are referred to this editor's checklist of Rossetti materials at the Library.[1] The letters from Leyland, and fragments A and C from Rossetti (in the Appendix), are in the special collections division of the Library of the University of British Columbia.

Annotations have been kept as brief as possible and are limited to matters of fact rather than of opinion, although there are necessarily some exceptions to the latter. Two abbreviations used often in the notes should be defined here. "L" designates the four—volume *Letters of Dante Gabriel Rossetti*, ed. Oswald Doughty and John Robert Wahl (London: Clarendon Press, 1965-67). Since the pagination is consecutive it

---

1. "The Rossetti Collection at the Library of Congress: A Checklist," *Bulletin of Bibliography*, 30 (July-September, 1973), 132-136.

has not been necessary to specify the volume number. "CR" refers to *The Paintings and Drawings of Dante Gabriel Rossetti: A Catalogue Raisonné*, ed. Virginia Surtees, 2 vols. (London: Clarendon Press, 1971). The number following "CR" is the catalogue number assigned to the painting by Ms. Surtees.

The letters are numbered chronologically. Leyland always dates his letters. Dating for Rossetti's letters sometimes depends upon internal evidence, but all conjectures are so designated. An appendix includes four letters or fragments which for various reasons do not belong in the regular sequence.

I am pleased to acknowledge the help of the staffs of the Library of Congress, the Library of the University of British Columbia, the Newberry Library, the University of Chicago Library, the Northwestern University Library, and the Loyola University Library. The Committee on Research of Loyola University awarded two research grants which aided materially in the completion of this book. I am grateful to Mr. P. W. G. Lawson, of the Merseyside County Museums, for very helpful information; to Dr. Frederic Faverty, for advice and timely encouragement; to Dr. Charles Hart, for criticizing the manuscript; and to Thomas Gniech and Joanne Saccomano, for help with proofreading. The Clarendon Press has kindly allowed me to quote from the Doughty–Wahl edition of Rossetti's correspondence.

Special thanks to Dr. William Fredeman for making the Leyland letters available to me, and for giving his permission, on behalf of Mrs. Imogen Dennis and the Rossetti trustees, for the publication of the Rossetti letters. Attempts were made through the British Consulate, the Freer Gallery, and other sources to locate heirs of F. R. Leyland who could assign permission for the publication of his letters, but no heirs could be identified.

A final word must be reserved for my wife Kay. No one knows better than I how inadequate words must be if I try to define or appreciate her help. But at least let me offer the "still small voice of gratitude."

Evanston, Illinois
January 7, 1977

LETTER 1

9th April 1866

16.CHEYNE WALK 1

CHELSEA

My dear Sir

As you continue to express a wish to have a good picture of mine, I write you word again[2] of another I have now begun,[3] which will be of my best.

The picture represents a lady combing her hair. It is the same size as the *Palmifera*[4]—36 X 31 inches, and will be full of material,—a landscape seen in the background. Its colour chiefly white and silver, with a great mass of golden hair.

The price is 450 guineas. The mode of payment (should you wish to have it) £150 down, 150 on my showing you the picture far advanced (or announcing its arrival at such stage, should you not be visiting London at the moment) and the remainder on completion.

Will you oblige me with a line by return of post, as I am giving you the first offer of this picture which no one has yet seen, and in case of your not closing with it, should wish to place it elsewhere at once.

I am, my dear Sir,

Yours faithfully

D. G. Rossetti

F R Leyland Esq

LETTER 2

30 April 1866
[letterhead]

My dear Sir

Thanks for your remittance for which I send receipt subjoined.

Since seeing you I have found it necessary, in order to get in all I want in the picture, to enlarge it 2 inches each way, making it 38 by 33 inches.

Very truly yours

D G Rossetti

F R Leyland Esq

Received of F. R. Leyland Esquire the sum of one hundred and fifty pounds on account of a picture in hand, of the price of four hundred and fifty guineas.

D G Rossetti

£150-0-0

LETTER 3

1st August 1866
[letterhead]

My dear Sir

I have forwarded the cheque to Smetham. Shall I keep the drawing for the present, or do you like to have it sent to you?[1]

When I last saw you, I wished to say something as to your picture, but thought it would be more easily stated in writing. It is this. I am now so well on with the picture that I should greatly prefer going ahead with it till finished, but for this purpose should need the remainder of its price (172-10S-) by the 28th of this month when I have a considerable payment to make, whereas the picture might probably be in hand for a month longer, especially as my health requires that I should soon leave town for 2 or 3 weeks. By the end of September however I should make no doubt of completing the picture & sending it to you, if the above arrangement as to payment will suit you, but otherwise I should have to work at other things for the present.

Will you let me have a line in answer to this, & believe me

Yours very truly

D G Rossetti

F R Leyland Esq

.

LETTER 4

3 August 1866

[letterhead]

My dear Sir

I have to thank you sincerely for your kindness and consideration, which happen to be of material service to me at this moment.

I have been rather uneasy ever since last showing you your picture, as I felt it to be for several reasons at an unfavorable stage, and I am sure you cannot have received a very advantageous impression of it. Nevertheless I have no hesitation in saying that when it reaches you (I trust not later than the end of September) it will be better than any picture of its class that I have yet completed, and I feel impatient that you should see it to more advantage than hitherto.

I send you the little Smetham drawing today by Passenger Train, and think I have got it packed quite securely without a case. I do not know whether you have seen Smetham's etchings of which I think Mr Miller[1] must have a set.

I heard Burne Jones speak yesterday of Solomon's Heliogabalus[2] as one of his very finest drawings. I have not yet seen it myself.

I am, my dear Sir,

Yours very truly

D G Rossetti

F. R. Leyland Esq

3rd August 1866

Received of Fred^k R. Leyland Esq the sum of four hundred & seventy two pounds ten shillings for the picture of Lady Lilith.

D G Rossetti

£472-10-0

LETTER 5

31 May [1867]

My dear Leyland

Thanks for cheque £105 on acct of Mrs Leyland's picture.[1] I think I have settled all the arrangement in my head now & that it will come very well—the picture goes today to be enlarged.

Many thanks for many coming feasts of oranges.[2]

Ever yours

D G Rossetti

LETTER 6

18 June 1867
[letterhead]

My dear Leyland

Would you oblige me with a further remittance of £100 on acct of my work in hand for you.

Mrs Leyland's picture is much advanced and in every way much altered, as I have again had it considerably enlarged! To begin a fresco as a pocket miniature seems to be my rule in art. The picture is now 29 X 21 inches sight measure. I propose to charge you the same price as the *Loving Cup* for it, though considerably larger than that.[1] The fact is, I regret having been forced at all to exceed without consulting you your original request that I would do you a picture corresponding with the *Carol*,[2] but the exigencies of the design have left me no choice in the matter.

I have now given the figure a flowing white and gold drapery, which I think comes remarkably well and suits the head perfectly. I think

I cannot do better than call the picture again *Monna Rosa*, and adopt a quotation from Poliziano,[3] which fits it happily:—

"Con manto d'oro, collana ed anelli,
La piace aver con quelli
Non altro che una rosa ai sua capelli."[4]

Thus the lady, richly dressed, is cutting a rose to put in her hair, & the treatment of the figure is accounted for.

With kind remembrances to the original & to yourself & hoping to see you again before long,

I am yours sincerely

D G Rossetti

F. R. Leyland Esq[5]

LETTER 7

Thursday [20 June 1867]

My dear Leyland

Thanks for cheque (£105) on acc[t] of *Monna Rosa*. I shall be glad to see you Saturday or Sunday.

Thanks for photo: which is so-so,—good but a little grim.

Ever yours

D G Rossetti

LETTER 8

16 Cheyne Walk
Chelsea
9 Sept 1867

My dear Leyland

I've been kept here till now, and just as I'm going I find there will be some money needed here on Friday next. I didn't mean to ask you for the 100 g[s] remaining on the "Loving Cup" till all your pictures reached you, but at this juncture would be obliged if you would kindly send here a £50 note by registered letter.[1] This will be quite enough. I have left directions for its use in my absence.

Excuse my giving you this trouble. I shall be away for a week or 10 days I suppose,[2] and on my return hope to see you soon.

Ever yours truly

D G Rossetti

F R Leyland Esq

LETTER 9

28th Dec 1867
[letterhead]

My dear Leyland

As usual with me, your kind reminder finds me stuck in a thicket of work; and even before your note came, a seasonable greeting, of baronial aspect, had reached me from Speke Hall,[1] with Mrs Leyland's superscription. Let me return such good New Year's wishes at once to both of you and to all your family circle, including my old friend Louisa Parke.[2]

As to New Year's Day, I must now confess I ought to have remembered that, although my mother only claims me at her own board on Christmas Day, certain aunts of mine always combine to ask all of us for the New Year unless, as sometimes, the family meeting takes place at my house. I know my absence would be a disappointment to my mother; and thus can only reckon on doing my best to meet you all some days later, respecting which I will write again when I have consulted with Howell.

Another point I must needs mention beforehand is this. Not long ago I and another or two proved fearful defaulters in a scheme for visiting Mr Rae[3] at Birkenhead; and I then engaged to give him primary notice of any incursion of mine into his neighbourhood. This too I should have remembered earlier. I should thus fear to displease him, as an old friend, were I not first to stay 2 or 3 days with him,—a little difficulty which I am sure you will perceive and appreciate. I now write in a scattered state of mind, but will collect my powers of combination by another post or two, and should be most reluctant to forego our arrangement.

With thanks and kindest remembrances

I am always yours

D G Rossetti

F R Leyland Esq[4]

LETTER 10

17th January 1868
[letterhead]

My dear Leyland

I remember you telling me to ask you when I needed the last 50 gs on the picture in hand. That critical period has arrived and I should be much obliged if you would send me the amount by return of post.

There is hardly anything to do to the *Lilith* now except the kitten, & the massacre of the feline innocents not having yet taken place, I have to wait awhile. The other two are substantially finished.

I shall be very glad to see you on the 22nd & all the gladder if I can then return with you. If not absolutely then, it will be soon after I doubt not, & the change will be a benefit to me. But just at this moment I am sunk deep in many miry ways of work & business. Venus[1] has got a face at last however ! ! ! ! ! ! ! ! !

Howell's affair about his cousin[2] has caused him the greatest vexation, but nothing would have relieved it so much as your kindness in the matter. I feel that I myself am not blameless in having helped to introduce him to you, but I see you are so well disposed to a general amnesty that I will not bother you with more apologies. Sad indeed it is to hear such a relation in one's family as this one of poor Howell's.

With kind remembrances

Ever yours

D G Rossetti

LETTER 11

18 January 1868
[letterhead]

My dear Leyland

Thanks for enclosure £55 completing payment for the 3 pictures I have in hand for you.

My own impression as to the sum due was the same as yours, but not being quite certain I thought it best to be on the safe side. However as we both thought so, I have no doubt so it is.

Ever yours   D G Rossetti

P.S.   I hope you'll dine with me Thursday at 7, and I'll get Howell.

LETTER 12

17th Feb 1868
[letterhead]

My dear Leyland

Here are the dimensions:

	Picture	Frame
Lilith	33 X 38 1/2	48 1/2 X 53 1/2
M. Rosa	28 3/4 X 21 1/4	33 X 40 1/2
Carol	17 1/2 X 14 1/4	22 3/4 X 25 3/4
L. Cup	25 X 17 1/2	34 1/2 X 26 1/2

If you want the 3 last named at once, I will do at once the very little remaining to be done & send them to you—will you let me know.

I have not yet thanked you for much succulence in the shape of oranges by which I have been profiting for more than a week past. My reason for not writing has been, as you may have guessed, that I wanted at same time to fix a day for coming to you. The demon Worry has so marked me for his own lately that this has as yet proved impracticable, but I live in hope of soon coming yet, & the bright looking days we have had make me often think of you and the Country.

I congratulate you on the "blessed change" you have effected in the case of Leighton's picture.[1] Is it to be at Speke or in London? I shall have to paint you some stunning composition—Medusa or other—to be properly represented among these heroes.

I have come into possession of a drawing of mine of which the photo: was always a favorite with you:—Lucrezia Borgia washing her hands.[2] I saw it at Christie's in Windus's sale,[3] & seeing things I should like to alter in it I bought it myself for 70 gs. I shall not show it till altered, but then shd like you to see it. It is quite a small affair.

With kindest remembrances to Mrs Leyland & Miss Parke

I am ever yours

D G Rossetti

LETTER 13

Monday [February/March 1868]

My dear Leyland

I've written to Ford & Dickinson[1] to bring the case & pack the 3 pictures & the framed sketches of Mrs Leyland on Thursday—so I trust they'll reach you that night or Friday morning.

In haste

Ever yours

D G Rossetti

LETTER 14

Saturday [February/March 1868]
[letterhead]

My dear Leyland

Your address is quite an excitement—a glory and a dream. One day I must indeed see it before long, but shall not just now, as our visit to Liverpool can't come off—Brown and Marshall[1] who were to have come with me have cried off—Brown because he won't come & Marshall because he can't, poor fellow, being ill with rheumatism.

I'm glad at any rate that we're to see you here again. Little to show though as far as I'm concerned. The only thing of any consequence done lately—a largish water colour²—having gone to Manchester.

Many thanks abt the Xmas Carol, which I shall be very glad to have as soon as you can conveniently send it.

Of course I never got away again till now after all & here still is [sic] & probably will remain.

Yours very sincerely

D G Rossetti

LETTER 15

Monday [9 March 1868?]

[letterhead]

My dear Leyland

When are you likely to be in town? I want to give you the first offer of the *Lucrezia Borgia* (size 17 X 10 inches) which I have taken up again, & which is coming very much to my satisfaction. You know I repossessed myself of it at the price of 70 gs for the purpose of making some alterations, & this has resulted (according to my wont) in completely taking out the figure and drapery and repainting it all from nature with a fresh turn of action given. It is now one of my very best things, & on seeing it you will agree with me that though small, it will be one of my cheapest at 120 gs. It will be finished by the end of this week, and will have taken me at least 10 days to alter, so I think I am fairly entitled to the profit on my purchase, especially as I cannot doubt, that, fetching 70 as it was before in the sale room, it must have fetched double now. I should like you to have it, as you have nothing better of mine, nor anything so distinctly wrought out as a historical subject; so I write to ask whether you will be able soon to see it, or whether you like me to consider it yours at the price named, before I offer it to any one else.

With kindest remembrances to all yours

I am yours sincerely

D G Rossetti

LETTER 16

20 March 1868
[letterhead]

My dear Leyland

Thanks for remittance—£157–10S-—in payment for Lucrezia Borgia & chalk drawing of La Pia.[1] I think you will not think it unreasonable if I charge you a "tenner" when I send *Borgia* home for the alteration you asked me to make; as the drawing is not yet finished & has taken me already longer than I anticipated when last writing you.

I got La Pia[2] on the canvas yesterday & the head will come stunning.

Ever yours

D G Rossetti

LETTER 17

11th April 1868
[letterhead]

My dear Leyland

I must write you a good piece of news, for does it not come through you in the first instance? Mr Graham,[1] whom you brought here, has asked me to paint him the "Dante's Dream" subject on a good scale—the design of which you have seen photographed over my mantelpiece.[2] He seems a very fine fellow the more one knows of him, & shows the kindest good will towards me & my doings.

By the bye, I am afraid I am going to bore you. I meant, before those chalk drawings went to you, to have had the 3 of Mrs Morris[3] photographed, and much wish to do so as otherwise I should not have liked to part with them. With many preoccupations, I inadvertently let Howell send them away before this was done. Would you mind letting me have them again for the purpose? I would gladly pay carriage, & you should be no loser, as now the lady is sitting to me, I would retouch the full-face one from her, as it was never quite finished. This whenever convenient to you.

I am trusting to see you again in a fortnight. If then you still fancy to have those rugs you saw here (as I think you seemed rather inclined to do) I have come to the conclusion that it will be wiser in me not to keep *them* but the money instead.

Ever yours

D. G. Rossetti

LETTER 18

16 Cheyne Walk
Wednesday [12 August 1868?]

My dear Leyland,

I know your friendly mind must have been alarmed by my seedy state when I was at Speke.[1] Since returning to London, I at once consulted an oculist[2] who assured me that my eyes were in no way diseased and also said he could guarantee that I should not lose my sight. Of course this allayed my anxiety in some degree, but I cannot say that the symptoms from which I suffer have abated as yet. I have been to another medical man about my general health, so that I have done all in my power.

I suppose now I ought to have a change, and indeed the medical men tell me I must go at once to the seaside and try rest and fresh air and walking. You will not I am sure misunderstand me, or think I underrate your friendship, when I say that I do not feel able to come to Speke again just now, as I am too nervous and worried to hold my own in any circle of friends, and to shut myself up like a bogie would increase my dumps. My brother says he will go away with me for a little while to the seaside, & this I believe will be my best course. I am anxious to start next week if possible.

Since being in town I have not been able to do much, but have finished your *Venus* drawing in chalk, as you told me you would like to get it. Shall I have it framed and send it you to Speke? At the same time I shall be able to send the other chalk heads (Mrs Morris) and the photos: I have so long intended to give you, as I have at last just received copies of some and am expecting others tomorrow. I will try also to send at same time the La Pia drawing of Miss W.[3] if I can get the background done.

I do not think you saw a watercolour of *Bocca Baciata* (which you may remember in oil.)[4] The watercolour can have been hardly in a state to show when you were last in my studio. It is much altered

12

in the head and hair from the original, and every one thinks it superior to that. It is much larger, being 18 X 15 inches. If you felt inclined to have it for 150 gs, it would be convenient to me at this moment, and you would find it quite equal to any small picture you have of mine, as it is decidedly one of my best watercolours. I could not I fear finish it to my satisfaction before I leave town, but I have brought it very forward and it only needs a few days work for completion. I had engaged it to Howell, but it does not seem to be convenient for him to pay just at this moment, and after all I may as well have the full price as he.

It is very possible however that you would rather wait for larger work, and I would not for the world that you had what does not meet your inclination. So I will trust to you to tell me quite frankly.

Will you give Mrs Leyland and the children my best remembrances, & the same to Miss Parke, and believe me

ever truly yours,

D G Rossetti

P.S. I should have written at once after seeing the doctors, only had hoped by a little delay to be able to report improvement.

LETTER 19

21 August 1868
[letterhead]

My dear Leyland

Thanks for your most friendly letter. Since I last wrote to you, some most fearful nights of unrest drove me to Dr Gull,[1] who said I was suffering from overwork and he would soon set me right. He prescribed for me, & I begin already today to feel my head unmistakably clearer & I think perhaps somewhat less distress in the eyes. Decided benefit in the latter respect, however, I do not yet feel, but am assured both by Dr Gull and the oculist (Bader of Guy's Hospl) whom I have seen again this morning, that there is absolutely no fear for my sight, but that I must rest and get change of air and scene for a time. I have conceived the idea of possibly, after a week at the seaside here, going to Germany and visiting the great oculist at Coblentz.[2] There also I could see my habitual doctor (John Marshall) who happens to be now at Bonn.[3]

Unluckily one of the most requisite things for such movements is wanting to me at the present moment,—to wit, money. I am very loth to trouble you for advances on work not yet fairly commenced; but some progress has been made in designs and studies towards the *Medusa* commission;[4] and I am constrained unwillingly to say that if you could let me have £150 on acc^t of this or the new picture I am to paint from Mrs Leyland[5] (whichever gets in hand first) I should be very glad just now, as I have no other way of managing what is necessary, and want to leave London in as few days as possible. If you can oblige me in this, a cheque will do now instead of sending notes.

I really hope to send the Lilith and Lucrezia very soon, and should have been taking them up lately, only that I find the last finishing of work is exactly what I am least able to do in my present state. I will attend to the sending off of the chalk drawings before I leave town, but the frames will of course occasion some delay.

I congratulate you on having got one of Millais' very finest works,[6] & hope that the Herbert was one ingredient in your "Scoop."[7]

With kindest remembrances to your family

I am ever yours

D G Rossetti

LETTER 20

Speke Hall
n Liverpool
24 Aug 1868

My dear Rossetti,

I enclose cheque for £150 on account of either Mrs Leyland's picture or the Perseus and Andromeda.

What your doctor tells you entirely accords with my own idea of your case; and you had better make up your mind to come down to [illegible] either before or after your visit to Germany.

I am glad to hear you intend soon taking up the Lucrezia and Lilith. I need not say how delighted I shall be to have them.

Truly yours

Fred. R. Leyland

LETTER 21

25 Aug 1868
[letterhead]

My dear Leyland

Thanks for cheque £150 on account of my next work for you.

So much benefit accrued from Dr Gull's prescription that I was in hopes of very rapid recovery. Today however I must say I do not feel so hopeful, but of course one must not expect miracles. I shall start for the seaside (perhaps Yarmouth) immediately and meditate for a few days on the advisability of going to Germany which is an undertaking & will not be necessary if I find myself getting well.

Ever yours

D G Rossetti

P. S. Six drawings will reach you as soon as frames are made: viz:
Venus
La Pia
Andromeda[1]
3 Mrs M.

LETTER 22

[spring 1869?]

My dear Leyland

I am sorry not to have seen you during the past week as Howell led me to expect you, & still sorrier to hear that the cause is some degree of illness,—I hope only a slight one.

I have been taking up the Lilith, which I think you said you hoped to get about the 20th of this month. I trust it may be ready by then, but am obliged for a few days after today to work at something else. I have painted a garland of silver flowers lying in the lap which is a great improvement, but am now anxious before sending you the picture to take out and entirely repaint (in the same colour) the pinkish brown drapery at the bottom of the picture. It has been so much altered as to be spoilt in execution. To do it again may cause a little delay in waiting till one can glaze it, but it is well worth while. You know we talked of having the frame altered so as to dispense with the black outside case, & have the glass within the frame itself. To do this properly would I find cost about £5. Do you care to have it done? I wish you would let me know at once.

Ned Jones's Circe[1] is finished & truly glorious. Watts has sent an *Endymion & Diana* to the R. A. which is a masterpiece.[2] Graham has bought it.

With love to all yours

I am ever yours

D G Rossetti

When do you come now?

Poor Jemmy Whistler! He worked awfully hard but failed to get his work[3] done in time.

LETTER 23

Speke Hall
n Liverpool
7 June 1869

My dear Rossetti,

I send enclosed cheque £200 acc. of Palmifera. Don't forget you promise *solemnly* to let me have this picture quickly. I don't like to bother you but you know how essential this one is to my happiness as well as to the furnishing of my house.

Get Lucrezia off your hands. She can be doing no good in your dirty studio.

Yours afftly

Fred R Leyland

LETTER 24

16 Cheyne Walk
8 June 1869

My dear Leyland

Thanks for £200 on account of the replica of "Palmifera."[1] This you may depend on my taking in hand as soon as possible, & on getting it infinitely sooner than "Lilith." How soon exactly however I may

16

succeed in finishing the original, on which the replica depends, I do not quite know as yet, but it will not I believe be very long. I believe it is likely Mrs Morris, who will be going shortly into the country, may be able to recommence sitting to me this week, for a short time. In that case I would not take up the Palmifera till afterwards, but meanwhile the replica can be carefully drawn in. Do not forget that you have to let me know the exact size of the Lilith. Or if necessary I can send some one to measure it.

When you made me an offer of 1500 gs for the Palmifera & Pia jointly, I had an impression that this was a reduction of 200 on my proposal. Contemplation and Cocker have shown me that 100 gs only is thus eliminated, and I accept your offer. Only I shall tell every one that the price of the Pia is 900 gs, (thus 1600 in all) and will rely on your not contradicting this little fiction. This being thus, I dare say you will let me have a second £200 cheque on the "Pia," as it is well begun. Thus we shall have (with the £150 I received from you in August last) £550 paid on the two works jointly,—one being well advanced, & the other, as a replica, promising speedy completion.

In selling the Pia I am in an obfuscated state as to the present law of copyright, & must therefore stipulate simply that I reserve all rights respecting it, as to engraving, exhibition, reproduction, &c.

Affectionately yours

D G Rossetti

F. R. Leyland Esq

LETTER 25

5 Oct. 1869

[letterhead]

My dear Leyland

I have been back a fortnight from Ayrshire where I was far from well, & whence I had to return rather unexpectedly. Since coming back I have found myself so walled up with things to attend to, that I really could not answer your kind letter with any certainty before this. All that I can say now is that I still think it possible I may manage to reach you before all fine weather vanishes, and that

I shall be only too glad if this proves the case; but I am too hampered just at this moment to feel certain about it.

I never got anywhere in Scotland except to my primary bourne at Penkill, and did not seem at the time certainly to be benefiting, but have felt somewhat better since my return.

I heard Jemmy's account of the doings during his stay at Speke, and of Fred's[1] determination to pay that Howell eventually in his own coin, on which I believe the image and superscription (which have puzzled many) are those of Ananias.[2]

If I don't after all see you at Speke, I suppose it will not be very long before London claims a visit from you on one account or another. I was delighted to hear from Whistler how completely set up you now are in health. I wish I could say the same of myself.

With kindest remembrances to all yours

I am yours affectionately

D G Rossetti

LETTER 26

16 Cheyne Walk
Tuesday [winter 1869-1870?]

My dear Leyland,

I had already heard with some consternation from Miss S.[1] of her extraordinary decision. However it is not hers but her father's. She was delighted beyond measure at your wish to buy, as old Brown (who first reported it to her from my report) told me before she got your letter. However when she showed this to her father, he said that the compliment on your & my part (considering the fine works you possess & my flattering opinion) was so great that he could not think of any other course but her offering the picture as a present & it was he who caused her to do so much against her own conviction. Indeed she was very uncomfortable afterwards & said she really feared you might consider it in the light almost of an impertinence.

I must explain to you that she *does* sell her works & is quite bent on adopting art as a serious profession, and that her father also takes this view most entirely. Only in the present instance (being an impulsive man) he seems to have felt so flattered by the incident as to have been driven on this extraordinary course. My own impression is that your best plan is to write a very serious note to the lady, thanking her duly, but saying that you really feel awkward and uncomfortable at so unexpected a result, and must venture to press her extremely to view the matter as you intended & accept the price of the picture, for which Brown I believe had advised her to ask 40 gs.

My promise (which I will strictly bear in mind) was to make you a *present* of a drawing in the event of a certain purchase. This was to be one of two, if I made two, or a duplicate of the one if only one was made. You may depend on my adhering to this in such event; and I will give you the refusal of any other such drawings with which I intend to part at all; but should probably keep one at least. Nor have I yet made any but shall I trust, as I am promised sittings.

I will write again about plans in answer to your kind inquiry when I know my chances of leaving.

Ever yours D G R

The sittings I had went in painting some hands.

LETTER 27

16 Cheyne Walk
25 Oct 1870

My dear Leyland

I had been expecting you in all likelihood to turn up in London for a flying visit, but I begin now to believe that the society of the great Jemmy makes you sluggish as regards pleasures far afield. I should otherwise have written to you before to tell you that I finished the last drawing of you[1]—putting a background and otherwise improving the tone of it, and that I am now very much better pleased with it, though it will be far from able to compete with the last labours to which Jemmy has doubtless been addicting himself to the like result.[2]

This week I determined that as I did not see you the drawing had better be sent off, and to that end was about to place it in the frame of the old one when lo! it (the frame) was not large enough. So I have had to order a new one which will be ready in about a week. Will you tell me whether you wish it sent to Speke or to Queen's Gate.[3]

19

I have worked chiefly on my big picture since seeing you, & have it so forward that I hope now soon to tackle the Medusa[4] also. I have got absorbed in the work & never gone away for any autumn change after all. I suppose it is now too late to be worth while striving.

Will you remember me most kindly to all at Speke, including Jemmy, & believe me

ever yours

D G Rossetti

LETTER 28

Speke Hall
19 March 1871

My dear Rossetti,

I shall most likely be up in town next week and can then go to the Dudley and look at Miss Spartali's picture.
We shall all be up in town in about ten days.

Yours ever

Fred. R. Leyland

LETTER 29

The Manor House
Kelmscott
Lechlade [late July 1871]

My dear Leyland

Do not curse me (though it wd be quite excusable) if I ask you whether there turns out to be any chance of your giving a trial at your office to the unlucky old acquaintance of mine whom I mentioned to you. I have collapsed you see into country leisure & am calculated to prove formidable as a correspondent.

This place is lovely & retired beyond exception, and in its modest way as genuine a relic of old times as Speke itself. It was originally built by the very family whose last living member has just ceased to reside in it. It is on the very banks of the Thames, & has an exquisite garden & other belongings, and Beauty & Peace are the names thereof. I am already beginning to recover from London, & wondering at my infatuation in ever living there. However it is highly probable that I now really shall never return to Cheyne Walk, as my studio is to be turned into a thoroughly satisfactory one during my absence by a radical alteration in the windows; so I fully expect that the great law of contraries will now keep my feet from it for evermore.

I suppose you too are all migrating from London now,—a favourable moment for congratulations & kindest remembrances.

Ever yours D G Rossetti

LETTER 30

16 Cheyne Walk
22 Dec 1871

My dear Leyland

I have kept in mind your last letter expressing a wish that I could let you have something finished by the time you next come to London. Therefore let me give you the first offer of a picture called "A Love-Song"[1] of which I enclose a sketch. I am getting on with it & mean to make it one of my best things. Its size is 34 X 27 inches. As you see, two ladies are playing music while Love holds a song-bird whose music chimes with theirs. Of course I need not tell you that the sketch is but the faintest shadow of the thing. I feel I am making advances now with every new thing I do, and I have no doubt of the picture pleasing you when finished. Its price is 750 guineas, and indeed, being a 3 figure picture, I think you will agree with me this price is not a high one; but I want to be working for you & not for another if it may be, as I have so long been wishing to send you something. We might transfer to this picture, in that case, the advance of £200 made on the abandoned duplicate of Palmifera, and thus lessen its still payable price by so much. I am working hard at the picture & should expect to send it you within two months, & thus, if you close with it, should, at this season of Xmas bills, be asking you for £400 on further account of it at once. Would you kindly let me know your decision, as no one has yet seen either picture or even design, & I want to settle its destination. I enclose the sketch in another envelope & will beg you to return it, as I may possibly find it of some service in working at the picture.

Of course I should like of all things to show you my big picture of Dante's Dream now, if you are ever in town. Indeed I should probably have written you before this of the picture being in a state to see, on the chance of its accelerating your movements townwards, but was deferred from doing so by the fact that every special appointment I have made to show it has been met by the clerk of the weather with such a careful provision of absolute darkness for that day and hour, that I tempt my fate no more in that way, as the picture cannot absolutely be seen except in a fair light, and one's nerves do not hold out forever under such onslaughts.

I believe I duly apologized at the time for breaking off our engagement about the Palmifera replica. But in fact I find these replicas more and more impracticable. I told you of my engagement to do one of Beatrice for Mr Graham.[2] This I attempted to carry out while in the country this summer & almost died of it, & even now I am still uncertain whether what I did will be available after all. New pictures for the future always, say I. Besides I know I am outgrowing my former self to some extent, as one should in ripening years, and had much better be doing new things only. I hope to be well *en train* with your large picture[3] almost immediately now, but have interposed this small one as a hors d'oeuvre during necessary loss of time in preliminaries. Every one who has seen the Dante's Dream (not yet quite finished, but close upon,) has seemed so thoroughly pleased with it that I think I may hope without vanity some progress has been made, & this I feel sure I shall carry on in my next work. Of course I have only shown the Dante to a few, as otherwise I might spend my time in nothing else, the picture blocking up the whole studio when displayed.

I have never yet written to thank you, as I should have done, for the brace of pheasants kindly sent through Howell. The delay has been simply owing to my wish to speak of these other matters at same time, & to get the Love-Song picture into a concrete state before doing so.

I dare say you saw my Epistle to the Philistians in the Athenaeum.[4] However they are bedevilling each other with mutual lying now in the most delicious style.

22

Will you give my kindest remembrances & all Xmas & New Year's wishes to your family & to Whistler, & take the same for yourself, believing me ever

affectionately yours

D G Rossetti

F R Leyland Esq[5]

LETTER 31

Sunday 24 Dec
1871

My dear Leyland

You will be astounded to get another letter from me before I receive your answer to my last. But I must not let Xmas Day pass without unbosoming myself, & hope you won't think me mad. The fact is that on tackling the Michael Scott subject, I find there are points in it which present unexpected difficulties for so large and important a work, and I want to substitute a Dante subject I have long had in contemplation. This would involve a good deal more work than the other, as it is an open air scene with a ship and many figures, but I shall be very glad to do it for the same price —2000 gs—if you will trust to me & make the change of place once more. I find I get so restless at working on anything else till my large work for you is fairly launched now, that I am disposed to put aside all question of the small picture I wrote you about & drop into this one and nothing else till I have it thoroughly under way. For that purpose I should have to ask you to make me now the same advance that Mr Graham did on giving me the commission for the work just finished—viz: £500. I would then get to it at once and give you a good account of it before long.

The subject is to be called "The Ship of Love,"[1] and illustrates Dante's sonnet at page 340 of my Early Italian Poets.[2] In it, Dante and his two friends[3] are in the enchanted ship, while Love brings Beatrice & the two other ladies[4] down the steps of a pier to join them for their love-voyage. I long ago made sketches for this composition, which has always been a great favourite with me, and am now irresistibly bent on painting it if you will favour my plan. I seem to want some open air subject, and this is a glorious one. The pier, river & city beyond, with the ship in the foreground and a row of children along the pier at the top of the picture, bearing branches for the love pageant, make a delicious ensemble and will I know bring out what I have in me. It will be a rather high-shaped picture, but not much more so than the Michael Scott.

So strong is the subject in my mind that I have set about getting a model of the ship made to paint from,[5] having got my authority from a beautiful one in a composition by Benozzo Gozzoli in the Campo Santo of Pisa. So (winds up my peroration) do say Yes.

Just as I was writing this letter, Dr Whistler has come in and told me of the trouble you are all in with the sad incident of poor Miss Gee's[6] death. I need not say how sorry I am to hear of it.

I dare say it will seem very capricious to you that I should have changed my mind about the Michael Scott subject, on which I was so hot 6 months ago; but ideas are sure to get superseded if they wait 6 months. This one shall—you willing—not wait a day, and I know I shall please you with it.

Affectionately yours

D G Rossetti

P.S. Former advances I will settle satisfactorily by finishing the picture of La Pia at the first pause I have to make with your large picture. Of course I need not state what you will clearly understand: viz: that if you greatly prefer the Michael Scott after all, I will carry that out as we agreed.[7]

LETTER 32

Speke Hall
26 Dec 1871

My dear Rossetti,

I was just on the point of writing to you to tell you how much I liked the sketch you sent me when I received your second letter.

I think the subject you now propose a very good one and from your description can quite imagine what a beautiful thing you will make of it; but before deciding whether it will suit me I must come up and see you about it which I hope to be able to do about the middle of January. The fact is I wish to know more about the size and scale of heads in the picture as in the Michael Scott picture I went to the extreme of height and this is an important consideration when pictures are merely used for rooms and not in a gallery.

I don't quite understand whether you feel indisposed to go on with the Love Song.

If so of course there is an end of it; but if you like to adhere to your first proposition and go on with it I will take it and send you the cheque you ask for on hearing from you. This of course would be independent of and in addition to the large picture.

By the bye what are you going to do for me instead of the Loving Cup of which you retook possession last year.

Poor Miss Gee's death has cast a sad gloom over the house and I should have been glad to run away for a day or two to town if I could have got away from business. I cannot however do so for two or three weeks yet.

Yours ever

Fred R. Leyland

D. G. Rossetti Esq

I return the *sketch*

LETTER 33

27 Dec 1871

My dear Leyland

I shall be very glad to see you about the middle of January & talk over the Dante subject. There can be no difficulty about the size. Even if it should be necessary to make the figures a little smaller than in the larger picture just finished, that would not matter; as, the composition being so full, it is desirable not to have the figures towards the top of the canvas too far from the eye. Meanwhile I would be obliged if you wd at once kindly send me the first advance of £500, as I am needing it, and am now ready to begin the large work for you, whichever we fix upon, though I feel no doubt the Dante will be the one. I had not spoken to you on this business point before, as I would not do so until the other large picture was off my hands & I was quite prepared to make a start with yours.

The little picture is getting forward, but I have made a great change with it. The figure of Love I found did not come in well when I came to study that part of the group from nature, so I have now introduced instead a couple of ladies dancing. These figures are seen full length in the middle plane of the picture, & fit beautifully into the space left between the 2 music-playing ladies, so as to give the picture, I think, a very new and graceful "motive." I am now calling the subject "The Bower-Meadow." If you like to have it in its new form, I feel sure still of its pleasing you—indeed I think it much improved by the change. In such case, I will ask you to send me £200 on account of it—making (with the advance on the large picture) 700£. If I do not begin the larger picture before I see you, I will probably have this small one in a very forward state by then, but want to settle its destination at once, as there is all sorts of need for tin just now, I assure you, with me, this blessed Christmas time. So if you will oblige me in the matter I shall be glad, and had rather you had the picture than another, as I have felt quite behind-hand with you, and you have long heaped coals of fire on my head by waiting so patiently while I worked for Graham.

Praised be the Gods, I feel something like growing strength for the work in me, for as worrying a world as it is in many ways; and if I can get some new things done now, they will be a precious deal better than any as yet, I know well. So you will not have been a loser at any rate in the long run by the delay. I want greatly to show you my big picture as I think it gives unmistakeable earnest of the advances I am making, & every one else seems to think so too, which is more to the purpose.

Why don't you give yourself the delight in life of building a fine gallery for big pictures? What a jolly thing that would be!— and you have capital space for it I should think at the back of your smoking room by some management, if indeed you feel sure of remaining at Queen's Gate. If not, then you could change your quarters with a view to such facilities. I know I'd do it if I were you, for what is life worth if one doesn't get the most of such indulgences as one most enjoys?

Ever yours

D G Rossetti[1]

LETTER 34

Speke Hall
^{n} Liverpool
28 Dec 1871

My dear Rossetti,

I enclose you a cheque of £700 on account of the work you are doing for me—to go either against the Bower Meadow (if I take it) *and* the large picture; or against the latter alone if I don't take the Bower Meadow. I wish you would go on with this latter so that I may see it pretty well advanced by the time I come up to town.

I shall be quite satisfied for you to put the Loving Cup against a pendant to the Lilith. What do you propose to charge me for the difference. If you put the pendant at your present scale of prices I suppose you will estimate the Loving Cup in the same rates.[1]

I am glad that you have got Graham's picture[2] out of hand, and that you can now begin to work for me. I confess that I have been all along sorry to have so little of your important work. However it is some consolation to know how much better your work is. I saw Palmifera the other day and went away oh! so wretched and unhappy.

Could you arrange for the Bower Meadow to be two or three inches larger each way? It would be a more suitable size as a decoration.

Yours very truly

Fred R. Leyland

D G Rossetti Esq

LETTER 35

Friday 29 Dec
1871

My dear Leyland

Thanks for cheque £700 duly received—being either £500 on the larger picture & £200 on the "Bower Meadow," or else wholly on the large picture if you do not take the "Bower Meadow." I am sorry I cannot oblige you as to the size of the latter, but the composition is an exact fit for the canvas & would not bear meddling with. It is one of those things which depends on calculated proportion —I dare say we shall manage to agree about the Loving Cup exchange.

When in town you *must* at last get the Lilith sent to me, as I'll make it in a trice much richer in tone than it is, now that it has long been quite dry. The Bower Meadow is going on well & shall be advanced when you come.

Ever yours

D G Rossetti

LETTER 36

4 Jan 1872

Dear Leyland

Can you tell me about what day to expect you in London, as I don't want just to be preoccupied at the moment you come? But I dare say you'll write one the day before. Is it likely to be in a week or a fortnight or what? The little picture has been rather backwarding itself lately, but I hope to recover lost time with it before I see you. The later the better, as far as this picture is concerned. Let me know when.

Ever yours

D G Rossetti

LETTER 37

25 Jany 1872
Thursday

My dear Leyland

Ever since I saw you I have been working very hard at an entirely new picture from the Palmifera model,[1] and it will be much the best I have ever done. The figure is mainly done except for last glazings &c, and I am going on with the thing like a house on fire. I don't know whether I shall not have to make it a few inches higher than the Lilith—indeed I think I shall. In width it will be but little over that I think. Its price will be 800 g^s—and you will see that it is not dear. Shall I consider it yours? In that case I trust to have it ready for you by the time you come to settle in town. The Lilith was sent here yesterday & I'll work on it as soon as I can. I believe I proposed to paint you a companion to Lilith for 700 g^s but when you see this you will agree I should have no difficulty in getting 800 for it anywhere. I think at present of calling it the Day Dream. The girl is in a sort of passionate reverie & is drawing her hand listlessly along the strings of a violin which hangs against the wall, while she holds the bow with the other hand, as if arrested by thought at the moment when she was about to play. In colour I shall make the picture chiefly a study of varied greens. I have not yet quite settled the background but am going ahead at it.

I think I shall have to return the Loving Cup & do what I can to make it more to my liking.

Now about the big picture. The necessity of making the figures so much smaller damps my ardour a little as to that Dante subject. You know, as I have often said, the subject of all subjects I want most to paint is that Cassandra one.[2] However, the lowest I could attempt to do it for w^d be 3000 g^s. Now suppose you give up the Bower Meadow picture & let me paint you the Cassandra, which will be much cheaper at the price I name than anything else at a lower price: indeed I am putting it too low, but want to do it and to do it for you without further delay. You see the increase of price will be but little over the Bower Meadow & the large Dante together, & the gain to you immense. As one figure does not stand much above another in this Cassandra composition, the figures could be made of a good size within your maximum height of 7 ft. I have in my head clearly all I mean to do with the picture, to which of course the old design you know for it will only bear the faintest relation. In case of such arrangement, we w^d consider the 200£ received on the Bower Meadow as an advance on the Day Dream picture (supposing you accept this.) If the Cassandra plan does not suit you, I shall put the large Dante in hand at once.

Ever yours

D G Rossetti

P.S.   On reading this letter over I feel inclined to say—I hope the proposal about Cassandra does not look like taxing you with a larger composition than we had agreed for. The fact is I have no doubt at all that Graham wd be glad to take it at the price named as soon as I could do it for him; but I do want to do it at once if may be, before I die or rot somehow, & therefore propose it to you.[3]

LETTER 38

Speke Hall
n Liverpool
27 Jany 1872

My dear Rossetti,
    You must abandon the idea of the Cassandra picture for me, as I have fully made up my mind not to go beyond a two thousand guinea picture. If therefore you are satisfied with the smaller scale of the Dante picture, go on with that; or, if not, then with the Michael Scott:—but don't let the height of either of them exceed seven feet—a few inches less would be all the better having regard to where the picture will be hung.
    As to "Bower Meadow" I did not intend to convey to you that I would take it nor in fact did I say so. On the contrary I found it too small to go with Lilith which was one of the principal things I had in view;—so that the £200 paid on this picture will as agreed have to go against the large one.
    I will be up in town in a fortnight or three weeks, when, if you have not already disposed of it, I can see the single figure picture. I may however as well say frankly that I should not be disposed to exceed the price agreed for for Palmifera—700 gns—so if you have a chance of selling it before I come up don't lose it on my account.

Yours truly

Fred R. Leyland

30

LETTER 39

Monday [26 February 1872]

My dear Leyland

One word to say that no missive of yours has reached me. Not that the matter is of any consequence before we meet again, but only in case of possible miscarriage, as I know your punctuality. By the bye, the picture is now so nearly done that I think I will ask you to let me have the whole outstanding sum on the picture —640£ together. Since you left, I think I have done wonders for the picture which I hope will really look well. When done so far, which will be I trust by your return this week or nearly so, I shall put it aside to dry and then finish it as regards glazing &c. in the frame which I have ordered & trust to have in a fortnight. Thus I make no doubt of letting you have the picture finished in less than a month from now, and hope to deliver the Lilith again about same time much improved.

Of course what I say about amount of cheque does not matter in the least if a cheque as at first settled happens to be crossing this.

Ever yours

D G Rossetti

P.S.   I will write on business points when I get the cheque.

LETTER 40

27 Feb 1872

My dear Leyland

Thanks for cheque £300 safely received on account of the picture of the Lady with violin.

I believe you will find our accounts now stand as stated overpage. I trust to be seeing you on your return to town—either Thursday or Friday as you please—& want to show you the picture which looks I think twice its former self.

In the opposite account you will perceive that I have transferred to acct of Lady with violin the £200 originally received on proposed replica of Palmifera.

Ever yours

D G Rossetti

£500

received on account of large picture from Dante
(price 2000 guineas)

£500

Received on Lady with violin (price 800 gs)

£200

Received on La Pia (price 800 gs)

£150

received on . . . . .

This we can place to account of La Pia or else of any next work I may do for you.

Ever yours,

D G Rossetti[1]

LETTER 41

[early March 1872]

My dear Leyland

How very kind of you to remember me again & send some more oranges! I hope to benefit more personally by these than the last, though indeed, much as I enjoy them, it is still pleasanter to give the enjoyment to any one to whom illness makes fruit the most important of indulgences. Having written that virtuous sentence, I perceive it is necessary to disclaim plagiarism from Goody Two Shoes or any other work.

I got the frame of your picture yesterday, & see exactly now what remains to do to it, which is a goodish deal—though no great matter as to change—in the way of glazing &c. But whether I can do it at this moment or not I am not quite certain, for the gilding of the frame is so unsatisfactory in colour—being a sort of dead bright yellow—that I verily believe I shall have to return it & get it altered. I suppose the maker w^d say I hurried him, but however that may be, it is not satisfactory. The gilding, I suppose, has been over sized.

The picture is so nearly done that I will ask you to send me the outstanding 340£. By the bye I may as well here formally notify the error in my last account sent to you. In reality the sum of £150 there remaining "unattached" should have been 350£.

Ever yours, D G Rossetti

P. S. I mean to call the violin picture "Veronica Veronese" which sounds like the name of a musical genius.

LETTER 42

Thursday
14 March 1872

Dear Leyland

Thanks for £340 completing price of the Violin picture. Will you come in on Saturday & see it in the frame which I have had somewhat doctored but I don't think it suits well.

Ever yours D G Rossetti

LETTER 43

16 Cheyne Walk
Friday [spring 1872?]

Dear Leyland

Many thanks for the oranges. I still hope to work at the Lilith, but did not (by what you wrote before) expect you here so soon, & thus am in the middle of other work which it is difficult to break into just now. If forced only, I will send your picture back as it is for the present.

Ever yours D G R

LETTER 44

9 Oct
1872

Manor House
Kelmscott
Lechlade

My dear Leyland

I am sorry you should have got the start of me in writing, as I meant shortly to have written you word when I had finished & delivered the Lilith. I am working down here (not in London) & have a model who just suits me for the complexion[1]—all that remains is to do it—so I shall soon be able to announce its completion. I have all appliances for work here, & am dropping into various pictures with a relish. I worked in Scotland too, but only on jog-trot work, having no models at hand.

While in Scotland, I did my best daily to walk off an obstinate & unaccountable lameness of the left leg, which however revisited & revisits, so that I still have a sort of hop & hobble with me. I shall probably be staying in the country, as my doctor strongly advises, & if I could find a suitable place nearer to town than this, might probably carry out my long-standing plan of settling in country quarters for good. However at present I am quite undecided. With the exception of the trifling lameness (which interferes neither with working nor even with walking, & so troubles me little) I am extremely well & all agog for work which will be my very best hitherto. I may be writing you more about it anon, & will let you know immediately when Lilith is done.

With kindest remembrances to all yours, & to Louisa Parke,

I am ever yours

D G Rossetti

LETTER 45

Speke Hall
n Liverpool
11 Nov 1872

Dear Gabriel,

I was glad to see you write in such good spirits, but I do hope that you wont be hidden away in such an unapproachable spot as

Kelmscott when I come up to London or I shall see next to nothing of you.

I have been most anxious and worried these last few months in disputes with my partners as to what is to be done on the approaching termination of our partnership on the 31st December.

However, I have at last carried my point and got quietly rid of them and they leave me in full possession on the 1st January when I shall hoist my own flag and carry on the business in my own name.

I know you will be glad to hear it; and still more that I have succeeded in dictating my own terms.

Yours ever

Fred R Leyland

Letter 46

2 Dec 1872   Kelmscott
                                    Lechlade

Dear Leyland

Today I send away Lilith, to which I have done a great deal. I will say that it is now a complete success, & quite worthy to hang with the fiddle picture.[1]

I have also finished here & to-day sent away your little Lucrezia Borgia.

The Lilith has gone to Ford & Dickinson, who must back it up & hang it at your house. The Borgia has gone to Howell, as it needs his special care, he having done the mounting all along. The frame of it is with F. & D. who will send it on to Howell.

I congratulate you on your success vis-à-vis your partners. No doubt it was a hard push, but I should have expected precisely this result, unless indeed you had transported them for life into the bargain.

Ever yours

D G Rossetti

Both Lilith & Veronica shd eventually be varnished (say by Merritt)[2]—I shd think in about a year's time.

Kelmscott   18 March
Lechlade   1873

My dear Leyland

To-day I am sending you your Loving Cup, which, as you will see, has benefited much by its stay with me, though I certainly never reckoned on that stay being so long an one. I thought the great improvement in the Lilith might probably draw a line from you whereby I might know of your advent in town; but I am aware how extremely busy you have been, and you on your side have probably been expecting to hear from me.

I have been steadily at work here all along and find no difficulty in getting my models from town. Miss Wilding is coming here immediately, & I propose beginning a picture or two from her instantly for your drawing rooms, of the same order as the Veronica, & I trust as rapidly successful as that, feeling, as I do, quite in the mood to make them so. I have several very jolly & suggestive instruments, & nothing could be more pleasant to do or to see together than several musical pictures.

I have here the large sketch for the "Dante's Ship of Love"; but the more I consider the subject, the more I find that, well satisfied as I am with the composition, the subject might not perhaps possess sufficient intensity of motive to carry one through in the execution of it with the same certainty with which I entered on the other Dante subject which I painted for Graham. A central tragic interest seems almost indispensable to inspire one for a leading work. I remember you repeatedly expressed yourself indifferent as to whether the sum (£500) paid on account of this picture when I made the design, went to this or other work eventually. I am quite resolved as to painting the "Desdemona's Death-Song",[1] & this would form a splendid centre for other musical pictures in your drawing rooms. Shall I view the matter in this way for you? The Desdemona will shortly be commenced. It would be less in price than the "Ship of Love." The figures would come (as we reckoned on measuring) of a moderate life-size, without interfering with its conveniently taking place over your piano.

I lately got a new & fine model & made a *nude* chalk drawing from her of a Siren playing on a wonderful lute, with a background of blown leaves and sea.[2] The drawing is a standing figure nearly to the knees, and is as fully coloured as an Italian fresco,—quite as fully, for instance, as the pictures by Moore which you have.[3] I am now finishing the background, and the frame (not an ordinary chalk drawing frame; but more a picture frame, as this drawing is quite a picture,) will be with me this week. The drawing is in size 30 1/2 X 21 1/2 inches, & would hang admirably with pictures. It is one of the very best things I have ever done—& is indeed like all I do & shall do now, better than any but the few last. Its price is 150 g[s]. If you like to have it, send me 100 g[s] & put the 50 to our account. The price is higher than I have yet asked for a drawing, but this drawing is, as you w[d] see at once, a picture.

I send this letter to London but don't know whether you may be there or in Liverpool.

With kindest remembrances to all yours, & to Miss Parke, I am

Ever yours

D G Rossetti[4]

LETTER 48

Speke Hall
n Liverpool
20th March 1873

My dear Rossetti,

I had hoped to have been able to run down to Kelmscott to see what you were doing, and then to tell you personally how much I thought you had improved the Lilith picture. But the fact is I have only been able to spend Sunday and Monday in London every time I was up and you can imagine how much occupied I have been.

Drop the Dante picture if you feel you should not care to go on with it. I am quite satisfied to take other work instead.

Howell told me you had something of this in your mind and thought of doing rather some pictures of the Veronica class. This would quite suit me and would come in much better with my scheme of decoration than the Desdemona picture.

The chalk drawing I would rather not be tempted with. I have [paid?] out so much money lately with my business that I wish rather at present to confine myself to the expenditure necessary for the completion of the commissions already given.

When do you return to London? or rather do you intend to come at all this season? The pleasant society I used to have, [unintelligible] up, by your absence.

Yours sincerely,

Fred. R. Leyland

D. G. Rossetti Esq.

LETTER 49

Kelmscott   25th March
Lechlade   1873

My dear Leyland

Your possible suggestion of visiting me here is a very pleasant & welcome one, only I should like to have you visit at some moment when I had really something in a favorable state to show, & would then try perhaps to get a friend or two besides to meet you in this wilderness & renew old chats once more. It would be really jolly & desirable.

I myself feel much the separation from the few familiar friends—few they were, as you know—with whom I kept up relations in London: but it is not impracticable to see them even here sometimes I trust, though I am sorry to reduce, though it be but by one item, your own friendly London circle. But as you know, I had long been but ailing as a Cockney resident, & I have no hesitation in saying that I have greatly benefited in steady health by this change to the country which I had so often projected: and one's belongings soon hem one in when one is addicted to regular work.

So I shall not forget your suggestion, but really write you word when there is some work to show you; & as this place will then I hope be in a more favorable stage as to season, you will see how well worthy it is of a visit even for its own sake. In its minor way it is as complete a thing as Speke,—very minor as that way is. I believe I shall be doing better things than heretofore, & am sure the country is conducive to thoroughness in one's work. To be shut up with a mull one has made, & nothing to soften it off, & no pleasant friends to make one remember there are other things besides one's mull in the world,—is a condition of matters which will, if anything can, force one to try & do one's best. I have been working assiduously at that Siren drawing since I wrote you of it, & must rather congratulate myself that you did not take it, as I have

38

put so much study into it that I shall have to raise the price![1] I hope you thought the Loving Cup improved. I couldn't do as much with it as with the Lilith, but still have bettered it considerably.

I judge from all I hear that your work must be very arduous and incessant at this moment, and only hope that you will not allow yourself to overdo it. You are strong in every way, but even strength may push its efforts too far. I hear that you are looking worn and overworked, but no doubt success in your aims will be the best medicine, & for that I fancy your friends may trust you.

Howell was here for a few days, during which I was whirled on such a tornado of lies that the things of this world have seemed shadows to me ever since. He keeps up the charm by frequent letters, and has told me the most wonderful stories (which you may have heard too) of his doings & sayings at the School Board, where his county has insisted on his representing the Catholic interest! This it seems brings him into collision with certain Geniuses, to one of whom he said that the sentiments he (the other member) expressed touching the damnation in reserve for unorthodox brats must doubtless be derived from the code of "a Hammersmith God,"—the gentleman in question being member for Hammersmith. Altogether he seems to be keeping the Board alive in a very unusual manner; and the other day he sent me one of their circulars where he was entered as Treasurer, and where no less than 15 initials (representing the diplomas of various bodies) were appended to his name! Don't tell him I mentioned this to you, for I rowed him about it and told him it was a great mistake, & that if I had seen his name so registered before knowing him, it wd have taken years to get over the unfavorable impression.

It seems he has managed to get rid of his beautiful Countess[2] before I painted her, which I am very sorry for.

Well, I hope it may not be very long before we shake hands here, & do not doubt that when it does happen, we shall soon find ourselves immersed in old subjects and feeling much as if we had talked of them the day before.

I hope all your family are well and enjoying themselves as much as people can in England before the year makes up its mind to mend its ways. My kindest remembrances to all of them, and believe me

Ever yours sincerely

D G Rossetti[3]

39

Kelmscott   22 April
Lechlade   1873

My dear Leyland

I am working on your Blessed Damozel drawing,[1] and find it should
certainly be framed with a gold flat—gilt oak—not white like your
others. It is carried much further than any of those—indeed worth
the whole lot of them—and should hang as a separate thing. I was
going accordingly to order a gilt oak frame for you, but thought I
had better just ask you first.

I am well *en train* with one of your pictures,[2] and believe it will be
quite as good as the Veronica or better. When I can show anything
I'll try & get you here.

Ever yours

D G R

P S Bravo to Fred's triumph in the Harrow match, I did not know he
was such a dab at racquets.[3]

LETTER 51

Kelmscott   23 May
Lechlade   1873

My dear Leyland

I am sending you today, by Passenger Train, the drawing of the
Blessed Damozel, which I hope will please you. It is as good a thing
as I ever did,—indeed it is so much better than the commencement
of the picture which I made some time back, that I have commenced the picture afresh from it on a new canvas, & shall have,
when you can spare the drawing, to borrow it for use in going on
with the picture.[1] This drawing has (like the Siren I did lately) a
degree of pale fresco-like colour in it, & should hang with pictures,
& indeed would well bear a more elaborate frame.

As I am well on to one of your pictures now, and have designed
a second, I would be obliged if you would send me 400£ on further
account. They shall proceed without delay one after the other, &
the first will I trust be no very long time in getting delivered.
These 2 pictures will be priced at 800 g^s each, unless indeed

the one I am about, & which has 3 heads in it, should prove on that account *much* more time-taking: I should then charge 900 g^s for it, but shall not do so unless such proves the case. Between these 2 pictures I propose to divide £400 of the 500 debt owing from me to you on account of the proposed Dante subject. Thus their price (if 800 g^s each) would be reduced to £640 each; & the present (requested) advance would be so much further reduction.

As the precise boundary line of a picture is (as you know) the last thing I settle about it when well advanced, I would be obliged if you would at your convenience send me the dimensions of the Veronica, that I may see how far these can be made similar in size, but I believe both must be rather larger.

I will bear in mind what you tell me of Saturday as your best day for a visit here. I hope Fred liked his Paris, which must be rather altered from ours at first acquaintance.

Ever yours

D G Rossetti

LETTER 52

Liverpool

28 May 1873

My dear Rossetti:

I have received your letter of the 23rd; now the drawing has also arrived all safe.

It is certainly one of the finest I have seen; and I have it hung up in my office with the other pictures where it quite holds its own. The only pity is so fine a thing should be done in so frail and perishable a material.

As to the two pictures you wish to do instead of the Dante I cannot of course say whether I will take them until I see them in progress and for that purpose I will run down to Kelmscott when you tell me they are in a fit state to shew.

The sight measure of the Veronica is 3 ft 6 1/2 inches X 2 ft 10 in:.

I have now so many pictures in the house that when these commissions are finished I shall have no room for more than the "Pia" picture and the two you now write me about. On those three pictures you have had £1050 which seeing the little progress made with them I think as large an advance as you can reasonably expect me to make. So I had better tell you frankly I would rather not pay more on account of them until they are nearer completion.[1]

Yours ever

Fred. R. Leyland

D. G. Rossetti Esq

LETTER 53

Kelmscott   30 Sept 1873
Lechlade

My dear Leyland

I thought for certain to have been writing you long before this, and indeed am quite astonished to think what a time has elapsed since we last corresponded. I wished to be able, when writing again, to offer you some finished or nearly finished picture, & am now in a position to do so. I believe Howell has mentioned to you a Proserpine[1] I have here, being an entirely new version (though resembling it in main design) of one which you saw in London, as Howell tells me. The present picture is vastly superior to that one, having increased area, new details, & being entirely re-studied as regards proportions. It is better both in beauty of face & figure & in beauty of colour. I painted it indeed purely because I was dissatisfied with the first, & wished to do full justice to the design, which I valued; and it has benefited a great deal by the repetition. No one has yet seen it, and it has been offered to no one.

If you like to have it, its price is 800 g^s, and we might arrange as follows as to payment. Howell tells me the little Lucrezia Borgia is smaller than you care to keep. I will take it back, if you wish, at the price you gave, which I think was 120 g^s, was it not? I would further put 280 g^s to my outstanding debt to you (thus making, with the Lucrezia, 400 g^s off the price of present picture) & would receive 400 g^s cash. The picture will be ready for delivery shortly; but I now wish to take it up again, after an interval, for last work.

If you like, I can send you, to look at, a pen & ink design for the Proserpine, made *after the picture you saw*, in order to settle my mind as to rearrangement; & which has been mainly followed in the picture I offer you.

42

I should add that I am sorry you do not keep the Lucrezia, which is really one of my very best small things.

I wish, by the bye, you would send me your *Monna Rosa*. I want to work on it again with a fresh eye as regards colour & effect, & will do it as much good as I did your others, I promise you,—of course in its & your interest solely.

With kindest remembrances to Mrs Leyland & to all your family

I am ever yours

D G Rossetti

F R Leyland Esq

LETTER 54

Speke Hall
n Liverpool
2 Oct 1873

Dear Rossetti,

Let me have the sketch of the Proserpine and the sight dimensions and I will then write you fully in answer to your last letter.

The Lucrezia is I know a good little picture but it is the only small picture I have and is completely swamped by the surroundings.

I understood you were about some work of same size as the Violin picture for me. Has that come to anything?

Yours truly

Fred. R. Leyland

To what station can I send the Monna Rosa?—

I have just this moment received Sandys Valkyries after some years of weary waiting. He has however made a very fine thing of it—by far the best I have seen of his.

LETTER 55

Kelmscott   4 Oct
Lechlade   1873

My dear Leyland

The right measure of the Proserpine is 48 1/2 X 22 1/4, & the frame is 7 inches wide, same as that of Lilith. I send you the pen-&-ink

design[1] by rail with this, as even without frame it is too big (as mounted) to go by post. It does not belong to me, so I must ask you to be kind enough to return it packed as I send it for safety. Since making the design, I have added details which do not appear in it or in the former picture,—some ivy in background, & an incense-burner on the foreground slab of grey marble. In *beauty*, the picture much exceeds the sketch. The conception of the figure is connected with the legend by which Proserpine (having fatally partaken of a pomegranate in Hades & so excluded herself from permanent return to earth which would otherwise have been granted her) was permitted to spend one half of the year in the upper light & the other half in the shades of her new kingdom. The background of the figure–half light half shade—can however be accounted for on natural grounds (as needed in painting) since the opening of a door or window in a dim place with clear light outside would of course produce such an effect. The whole tone of the picture is a graduation of greys—from the watery blue-grey of the dress to the dim hue of the marble, all aiding the "Tartarean grey" which must be the sentiment of the subject. Proserpine looks yearningly towards the momentary light which strikes into her shadowy palace; and the clinging ivy which strays over the wall (in the picture) further suggests the feeling of Memory which indeed might equally be given as a name to the picture. It is a very favorite design of mine, and I have composed a Sonnet for it both in Italian & in English. The former appears on the cartellino in the upper corner of the picture, & the latter on the frame below. There is nothing dismal or gloomy in the colour & lighting of this picture,—a tendency to such defect in the first picture having been one of the reasons which determined me to repeat it. The whole is meant to have a mystic luminous warmth such as we find in moonlight effects, & I believe I have succeeded.

My reason for not writing you before about this picture was that I did not consider myself at liberty to offer it anywhere till I knew that the dealer (Parsons) had disposed of the other version, as it might have seemed an interference with his market.

In reply to your question about other work in hand,—when I last wrote you I made you a proffer of 2 pictures, one of which (La Ghirlandata) was chiefly occupying me at the time. I however needed the advance which I proposed; & as I could not continue to press the matter after your objection, I accepted an offer from another quarter of the whole price of the picture down in advance; & having accepted this I was of course bound to complete the picture before other things. It is now finished & delivered. It is a much finer thing, my dear Leyland, than the Palmifera which you always regretted to have missed; & it should have been yours if my plans had held good. Of the second picture I trust to make a work fully equal to the first. This I have cartooned from nature and am now beginning to paint it. It is called *Dis Manibus*,[2]—the dedicatory inscription to the Manes, the initials of which (D M) we find heading the epitaphs in Roman cinerary urns. In the picture, a lady sits in the "Columbarium" beside her husband's urn which stands in a niche in the wall, wreathed about with roses & having her silver marriage-girdle hanging among them. Her dress is white—the mourning of nobles in Rome—and as she sits she plays on two harps (one in her arm & one lying beside her) her elegy addressed "Dis Manibus." The white marble background & urn, the white drapery & white roses will combine I trust to a lovely effect, & the expression will I believe be as beautiful & elevated as any I have attempted. Do you like me to consider this picture as yours at 800 g^s? I should not be able to put so large a proportion of the price to back debt as in the case of Proserpine; that picture being mainly done & this one to do.

I suppose my chance of seeing you this year is over, in this worsening weather & with your London migrations long ended now. I wish we had met, but fate was against it.

Ever yours

D G Rossetti

P. S. Some time ago I told Ford & Dickinson to send & take a rubbing of the pounced pattern on the flat of the Veronica frame. I told them to do so while you were away, but if by chance they have not yet done so, will you kindly allow their messenger to take the rubbing still at some convenient moment, as they are making a frame for me in which it is required.[3]

LETTER 56

Speke Hall
n Liverpool
8 Oct 1873

My dear Rossetti,
    I have received your two letters 30 Sept and 4 Oct also the pen and ink drawing of Proserpine which I return to Lechlade station.

I must say I am disappointed at what you say about La Ghirlandata for I understood that was one of the two pictures you were to do for me instead of the large picture; and seeing the large amount you have already had on account I dont think you could reasonably expect me to advance any more until the work was well on to completion. However it's no use saying anything more on this point and we had better be understood as to how the affair is to be arranged.

As I have already told you I do not wish to spend more money in pictures than I have engaged myself to do—that is 2300 guineas for the Perseus and La Pia, against which you have received nearly one half—£1050.

I am willing to take the Proserpine and the Roman Widow at the price you name (assuming this latter is of the same size as the Veronica and that I like the cartoon which you can no doubt send down here).

What I propose is that to each of these pictures one third of the advance is placed; the remaining third would go to La Pia or (if it makes no difference to you) to an upright picture of the same size which would suit my arrangements better than an oblong picture as La Pia is. I would thus have to pay you

for Proserpine		£840
less Lucrezia	126	
advance	350	476
		£364
and for the Roman Widow	£840	
less advance	350	
	£490	

I fear there is no chance of my seeing you this year and I am sorry for it, as I would much have preferred to tell you all this by word of mouth because I could then have put the matter more delicately and with less fear of giving you pain, though at the same time I must candidly tell you I feel more disappointed than I can express at having none of your work long ere this.

I will send you Monna Rosa whenever you wish but don't send for it until you want to commence working on it. If you send the cartoon of the Roman Lady you had better send it to my office 27 James St Liverpool.

Yours very truly

Fred. R. Leyland

D. G. Rossetti Esq.

46

LETTER 57

My dear Leyland

I feel, as you do, an awkwardness in prolonging business correspondence, when by word of mouth an understanding would doubtless be come to at once.

I do not quite understand your last letter. You speak of our engagements "for the Perseus & La Pia" at 2300 gs jointly. But all question of the Perseus (price 1500 gs) had long ago been superseded between us by the large Dante subject substituted for it at the price of 2000 gs; which, jointly with La Pia, makes 2800 gs, if 800 gs was the price of the latter[1]: I am sure it was not less, but cannot quite recall exactly at this distant date without reference which you perhaps have at hand.

However, as regards this Dante picture, you said from the first that, if I ultimately preferred painting smaller pictures to the same account instead of the one large one, this would suit you equally well.[2] Later on (20th March 1873) you write me again: "As to the Dante picture, if you feel you should not care to go on with it, I am quite satisfied to take other work instead. Howell told me you had something of this in your mind, & thought of doing rather some pictures of the Veronica class."

In pursuance of this last plan I offered you in May of this year La Ghirlandata and the Roman subject,—the first to be 800 or 900 gs as the case might prove; the second 800 gs; thus leaving 400 or 300 gs of the original commission for the large picture still to carry out in some form.

As for La Ghirlandata, which has 3 heads in it, you will remember that you thought, on hearing this, that the picture would not suit you or correspond with the pictures that had to hang with it; and this objection being added to my inability to undertake the work without an advance, I accepted Graham's offer for the picture. I should have liked you much to have it at the time, having planned it for you, and wished much to be at work for you after so long an interval; but having more than one reason (as above) to believe my offer of it did not suit you, I had no choice but to transfer it. I could not have begun a fresh work for you, instead of the Ghirlandata, with funds only in perspective: nor can I indeed put aside a work at all when I am embarked in it & it interests me, unless stopped by obstacles in the work itself.

The last time we spoke of commissions at Queen's Gate (about the end of 1871) your views were to have 7 more pictures of mine, —viz: a large one & 2 smaller ones for the place over the piano in the back drawing room (which we measured at the time)—2 of the smaller size to face these, & 2 similar ones to face my 2 in the front drawing room. You had so decidedly said that you wished the drawing rooms to contain eventually my work only, that I had not doubted the continuance of this plan (with whatever modification of details) till I got your letter of 20th May 1873. If the scheme is now so entirely altered, this must of course render it much more difficult for me to restrict myself during any long time together to my work for you, when past advances have to be levied on so much smaller a commission in the aggregate than I had anticipated; and when I should thus be receiving such greatly reduced supplies from it. I should never have ventured to increase the advances already made by the last sum of £500 (on the Dante picture in Dec: 1871), had I not believed that the aggregate amount of commission made it safe for me to do so. It is unavoidable for me to refer here to this past matter (which I should not otherwise have done at all) in order to explain my present position.

Let me now reply as to the Proserpine & the Roman picture.

The former I have taken up again to finish, & it will be ready for delivery before very long, but I cannot say when *exactly*.[3]

As to the latter, I could not send you the cartoon which is too large & moreover only shows the figure from nature (Miss W.) & not the composition. I send you by rail a pen-&-ink sketch,[4] but it is rather a rough affair, done before going to nature,—however it will give you an idea of the general arrangement & in some degree of the effect. Of course it looks a deal blacker than the picture will, & lacks some details, accessories, &c. I find I shall be introducing some colour in the flowers & marble background.

The size of this picture will be almost exactly that of the Veronica; but as far as I can judge as yet, it is likely to be about an inch less in height & a couple of inches more in width. You know however that exact boundaries are among the last things I settle in a picture.

This letter is dismally long, & my only excuse is that it cannot be more dreary to read than to write. Again I wish we were talking

48

things over instead,[5] as we have so often done to speedy & satis-factory result.

With kind remembrances

Ever yours

D G Rossetti

F R Leyland Esq

LETTER 58

Speke Hall
Liverpool
20th Oct 1873

My dear Rossetti,
I have received yours of the 17th and return you the sketch of the Roman picture by rail. I like the sketch and am willing to take the picture.

I quite understand that the commission for the Perseus picture is at an end by substitution of the Dante subject, but that I also understand to be at an end; and I only referred to the price of the Perseus & La Pia as indicating the sums to which I originally committed myself and felt myself engaged. I quite recollect the conversation at Queens Gate but nothing was arranged and I never dreamt you were counting on this in asking the advances you did. On the contrary all your advances were asked against specific pictures commissioned and agreed for; and the advance of £700 in December 1871 was in your letter distinctly asked against the Dante picture and "Bower Meadow" jointly or if I did not take the latter then against the Dante picture alone.

No one knows better than yourself how much I like and covet your work and how glad I should have been to have my walls covered with it—but I long ago lost all hope of that.

The price of the Pia was as I said 800 gnas—our arrangement was 800 gnas for Pia and 700 gnas for Palmifera:—the latter you did not go on with much to my sorrow.

Yours truly

Fred R. Leyland

D G Rossetti Esq

49

Kelmscott   4th Nov 1873
Lechlade

My dear Leyland,

I should have answered earlier, but that I wished, when doing so, to say with some precision what time I expected the Proserpine should be ready for delivery. I find as usual, however, that on taking up the picture, unexpected work presents itself; and though there will be no great delay, I had better not defer writing longer.

I note all you say in your last letter, and should be above all things pained if you retained any impression that I had neglected your work. I have had from you both friendship and appreciation; both are rare, and I should wish to show that I am not unmindful of them. As thus. For some time I was obliged to work at Graham's large picture till finished. I then painted you the Veronica, which you accepted, and offered you the Bower Meadow, which you declined. Next I spent some 6 weeks in designing the large Dante subject for you, which design proved more loss to me, as I found I did not like the subject well enough to offer it to you after all. Then supervened illness, during which I worked for no one. Shortly after settling here, I offered you the Ghirlandata, but this again you virtually declined. Now that I am free of it, I am again offering you work.

Thus, since finishing Graham's large picture, *I have painted nothing of a leading kind which has not first been offered to you,*[1] except indeed Parson's Proserpine, & of that I am offering you the subsequent & better version. At intervals during the above time I have done my best to make former work more worthy of your possession, though the discontent with it was on my side only; and in working on the Lilith, Loving Cup, Lucrezia & Blessed Daml, I must have spent two months or nearly so. I mention all this not from the business side of things, but because it would really pain me if you thought me neglectful. Did I feel myself to have been so, I would say so promptly, as in any case it could only have been owing to stress of circumstances, but if you consider the matter as above, I think you will admit that there has been no neglect on my part, though the time which has elapsed must almost necessarily make it seem so at first sight.

I judge we are now agreed that you take the Proserpine, Roman Widow, & La Pia, (or substitute as I may be able to decide) at 800 g^s

each, & levy my debt to you in equal proportions on the three. When proposing to take back the Lucrezia, I was still under the belief that the sum in question as commission between us included the whole price of the large Dante subject. As your view is otherwise, I think you will agree with me that I cannot afford to mulct by a further sum of 120 g^s the price (already so curtailed by debt) of a picture which has cost me such unusual trouble as this Proserpine has, and which is certainly as good a thing as any of mine. I therefore propose that under these changed conditions we drop question of the Lucrezia. Living out here, I should not have its disposal ready to my hand, & cannot afford to be lacking the money.

With your sanction, I shall be delighted to paint you the 3 pictures, I hope without much delay, & most of all pleased if they please you when done.

Ever yours

D G Rossetti

P S As to the proposed Palmifera replica, I abandoned it in your interest, after I found myself, in spite of much labour, unable to reproduce the Beatrice for Graham to my own satisfaction.

About the Monna Rosa, I'll try to send for it only when ready; but the fact about such jobs is that if, when one is ready, they have to be sent for, one finds oneself sucked into some other job before they arrive.

LETTER 60

Liverpool
20th Nov 1873

My dear Rossetti,
I have been putting off writing to you from day to day intending to write you a long letter but have been so much occupied that I now find to my horror that my answer is a fortnight past due.
I had better therefore say shortly that I am quite willing to let the arrangement stand as you wish in your letter now under reply. At the same time I hope you will find yourself in a position to go on with the pictures until finished for as you know I have waited long for them.
From your letter I rather judge that it would be more agreeable

to you if the amount of the debt had to be spread over a large number of commissions. If this be so, I am willing that the Proserpine should be treated as a separate matter; that the payment should be as you first proposed (120 gns off for the Lucrezia and 280 gns off the debt) and the remaining portion of the debt should then go equally to La Pia, the Roman Lady, and another picture same size and price as the Roman Lady.

In the answer please suit your own convenience, only let me know what you decide.

Yours truly,

Fred. R. Leyland

LETTER 61

Kelmscott   22 Nov 1873
Lechlade

My dear Leyland

Your present proposal is quite satisfactory to me.

Thus, on delivery of the Proserpine, (I trust almost immediately) I shall receive the Lucrezia & £420. After this, a debt from me to you of 748£ will remain to be paid off in equal proportions on 3 800 guinea pictures, viz: La Pia, Roman Lady, & a companion in size to Roman Lady; making a reduction of nearly £250 on the price to be paid by you for each picture. This is correct, I think, is it not?

No doubt you intend that the payments should proceed on our usual plan hitherto,—that is, that I shall make calls when I need supplies; I undertaking on my side that the works shall always be progressing steadily while such calls are made.

I think I would prefer if you would get the Lucrezia sent to me *here*. Also, if you can now send me *at once* the Monna Rosa, I think I could undertake to return it you at same time with the Proserpine.

Ever yours

D G Rossetti

Had I better forward Proserpine (& Monna R. if accompanying it) to Speke or to Liverpool?[1]

LETTER 62

Speke Hall
n Liverpool
24 Nov 1873

My dear Rossetti,

I have received your letter of the 22nd which quite states my view of our present arrangement as to pictures. I shall be glad to pay you money on account of them as they progress towards completion.

I have today sent you by passenger train the picture of Monna Rosa. You had better send both it and the Proserpine to me at the office 27 James S^t; though I shall afterwards send the latter to London.

Yours truly

Fred. R. Leyland

D. G. Rossetti Esq.

LETTER 63

Kelmscott   26 Nov 1873
Lechlade

My dear Leyland

Your last letter to hand, concluding arrangements.

I would be obliged if you would now send me £200 on account of the Proserpine, which will reach you without fail in about a fortnight, or perhaps 3 weeks. I might have sent it much sooner, it having been at one moment substantially finished; but I saw my way to better it,[1] & it will be much the gainer by the delay, which will not be more than I say.

Ever yours

D G Rossetti

Monna Rosa to hand.

LETTER 64

Kelmscott   30 Nov 1873

My dear Leyland

Thanks for £200 received on acc^t of "Proserpine" picture.

Ever yours

D G Rossetti

I w^d be obliged if, at your convenience, you w^d have the Lucrezia drawing sent here, as I wish to set about disposing of it.

LETTER 65

Kelmscott   Wednesday
Lechlade   3 Dec: [1873]

My dear Leyland

Having finished working on Monna Rosa, I may as well return it you, as its place is probably an unpleasant gap on the wall. It leaves me tomorrow for 27 James Street. You will notice a radical change in the colour; but I am so sure myself that it is an immense improvement that I feel no doubt of your thinking so too.

Ever yours

D G R

LETTER 66

Kelmscott
Lechlade   19 Dec: 1873

My dear Leyland

On Monday I reckon for certain on sending you the Proserpine. It is my best & I hope will please you. It is essential that it should be placed in the light in which it was painted,—i.e. with the light from the left (left of spectator.) I hope you will find a light of this kind for it both at Liverpool and at Queen's Gate, as I should be sorry for it to be hung otherwise.

Please, on receipt of it, kindly remit me remainder of its price, and

I would be obliged if you would add £200 on account of the Roman Widow picture which is now well in hand.

I have not been able to get the title & English sonnet written on the frame, as Dunn was too busy to come down here just at this moment. But I propose (as you speak of sending the picture shortly to London where it would be useless at present) that you return it to me here instead when done with at Liverpool. It would then be perfectly dry by the time I sent it to London (whenever you directed me to do so) & would I have no doubt be the gainer by a few last glazings which cannot be added till a picture is as dry as a bone. I would then also get the inscriptions added to the frame.

Ever yours

D G Rossetti[1]

LETTER 67

Kelmscott   22 Dec: 1873
Lechlade

My dear Leyland

The picture is leaving here today by Passenger Train for 27 James St.

Will you take care
1st that it is lighted from left of spectator
2nd That you do not look at it first by lamplight, since its colour is finer by daylight
3rd That when the strips of paper are removed from the glass, the paste is also thoroughly removed & the glass well cleaned. This is rather a delicate job, as the paste is apt to leave a residue and cloud the view of the picture.

Please do not send it to London before you need it there, but return it to me meanwhile. It will probably gain something here; and besides that, I have a particular reason (connected with the Parsons picture) for not wishing this one to be sent to Marks (who I think is a sort of partner of Parsons) for a month or so to come.[1]

Ever yours

D G Rossetti

Speke Hall
Liverpool
26 Dec 1873

My dear Rossetti,

Proserpine has arrived but an awful smash. Luckily the picture has but trifling injury, a slight scratch on the neck and cheek being the most serious.

The frame however will have to be regilt and repaired. Evidently the case has had rough usage but the Railway Co are not liable for more than £10 on pictures unless you pay a special rate for them. However this I fancy will cover the damage. The glass was so heavy (being as I think about twice the thickness necessary) that the paper would not hold it and it was all knocking about the case. The wonder is the picture was not cut to pieces. I would recommend you never again to send a picture of this size by rail with glass on.

The picture goes back to you today. I have only seen it in the dim light of a Railway station so can say nothing of its beauty save that the general effect pleases me very much. I shall be anxious to hear that you have received it and what you think of the damage. I shall be going to London so soon—beginning of February—that it is useless sending it down to Liverpool again. You had better therefore do all you require to do and then send it up to town when I arrive.

I enclose cheque £220 to complete its cost; and I also send you check for £200 on account of Roman Widow.

This latter I send on the assumption that you are now going on with the picture.

Yours truly

Fred. R. Leyland

D G Rossetti Esq

LETTER 69

Kelmscott   Monday
Lechlade   29 Dec: 1873

My dear Leyland

I am just back here from my Xmas in London. Your letter & the

56

returned picture are indeed matter for consternation. I will write further tomorrow.

The two cheques safe to hand: viz: £220 completing payment for Proserpine, & £200 being first payment towards Dîs Manibus.

Yours ever D G Rossetti

LETTER 70

Kelmscott   31 Dec: 1873
Lechlade

My dear Leyland

I have now remedied the injuries to the picture so far as to render its complete restoration a certainty: but it will need to dry for a few weeks before I can completely unite the work. I have no doubt it will be quite ready by the time you need it.

With best wishes for the New Year,

Ever yours,

D G Rossetti

LETTER 71

Kelmscott   1st Jan:
Lechlade   1873 [actually 1874]

My dear Leyland

In writing yesterday, I forgot to ask—are you claiming compensation from the Railway Compy? Some one should surely do so, & you are more imposing than I. I am assured that, though the railways stick up placards to the effect that they are not responsible, they can be made so. Morris & Co. always make the porter wait while parcels are unpacked & have repeatedly made the railways pay for broken stained glass.

You see, our packing was not in fault in the least. Nothing stirred but the rebate of the little moulding in which the glass is inserted, & there must have been very rough usage to cause this, since all my frames are made alike, & I have repeatedly sent similar ones about from here safely,—your Lilith for instance. Lately the Ghirlandata—a larger picture than this—went safely from here to Scotland

and then to London. The glasses cannot I believe be thinner if of a good kind,—moreover there is a great advantage against ordinary accidents in a thick glass.

Ever yours

D G Rossetti

Moreover, how long was the thing on the road? It was sent on Monday the 21st[1] ult: by Passenger Train.

LETTER 72

Kelmscott	31 Jan:
Lechlade	1874

My dear Leyland

The Proserpine shall reach you in time. If you like I can send you another picture with it! As thus.

Last Spring I painted a picture for the special purpose of meeting a money call then uncertain in date but which is now coming due. Accordingly I never offered the picture anywhere at the time, or the money should have got spent before the call. For this reason it would be necessary that I should receive the price of this picture—700 guineas—*intact and independent of other commissions*, in case you like to buy it; as the money would all have to go as above.[1]

I shall call the picture either "Spring Marybuds" or "The Bower Maiden."[2] It represents a young girl (fair) in a tapestried chamber, with a jar containing marybuds (or marsh marigolds, the earliest spring flowers here,) which she is arranging on a shelf. Near her is a cat playing with a ball of worsted. The picture abounds in realistic materials & is much like the Veronica in execution & not inferior to that picture in colour. I never made a pen-&-ink sketch of it—the whole depending, like Veronica, on direct painting from nature,—thus I cannot send you such sketch to look at: but you would be quite certain to like the picture & it would be a general favorite. Its size is 44 1/4 X 28.

I offer it you before any one else sees or hears of it, in pursuance of what I said in a former letter regarding work done here up to our late correspondence. Please let me know your decision at once, as in case you do not care for it, I shall dispose of it elsewhere without delay. It is cheap at 700 guineas.

58

The Roman Widow progresses & will be as good a thing as ever I did, but takes time & trouble.

Ever yours

D G Rossetti

LETTER 73

Kelmscott   2 March
Lechlade   1874

My dear Leyland

I am sorry you have not been able to hang the Proserpine with my others in the drawing room. Works by the same hand gain so much when together. I judged you would put one of the 2 already there on the opposite side & hang this in its place, as it needs left-hand light more than they do.

I had better now tell you a long story which you would have had before but for its lengthiness.

Should you be surprised to hear that this picture is *not* the same which went to Liverpool & had the accident, but *is* the same I originally sold you? To explain.

When I had sold it you & took it up for last work I noticed for the first time accidentally what I had not become aware of before,— that is, that some threads of the canvas showed disagreeably in the face (though only when the picture was placed in the *wrong* light)—and this owing to the picture having been lined, which had made these threads prominent. I felt so discouraged about it that I at once began a replica and at the same time sent for the canvas-liner here to look at the picture. The result was that he took it with him to re-line it, and that I, carrying on the replica, became so convinced of its superiority in every respect to the other that I determined it should be yours instead & sent it you. The accident caused it to come back to me at the same time that the re-lined picture reached me in a greatly improved state as to the threads in the face. I then perceived to my astonishment that the re-lined picture was decidedly preferable to the other in brilliancy of colour & therefore set to work on last finishing of it & finally sent it to you. The threads in question *never* showed in the light in which I painted it, & are now little observable even in the wrong light. It is a pity they are there, but the fact is that almost every *old* picture has such inequalities which are never noticed. As you have hung it, they are quite invisible.[1]

By this explanation you will perceive that the frame is *not* the one which went to F. & D. after the accident. That is now on the replica which is still here, your picture being 2 inches taller than the replica. That frame has now had a moulding of double thickness placed to hold the glass in: and the same should be done to your Proserpine frame & to all frames of the same class, as otherwise the jolting is likely to shake the glass out. I may add that the injured picture has been set quite right.

You must not suppose that if the accident had not caused the 2 pictures to be confronted by me, you would not eventually have got your present one. On receiving it, even in the absence of the other, I should have perceived its superiority, & have written to make the substitution.

Thus there are now 3 Proserpines in existence. If you hear ever of the 2 others *de par le monde*, you must distinctly understand that yours is the flower of them. It is my very best picture, unless possibly the Ghirlandata might dispute the title with it; but I believe the Proserpine to be *the* best.

There is no human likelihood of the Roman Widow delaying to reach you beyond June. I would say it was sure to reach much earlier were it not that the vicissitudes of art render such undertakings unsafe. However you may be *quite* sure of June. I am glad you have got so favorable a house for pictures as the one Lord Somers used to inhabit. There all will be well.

I hear that Legros has some very fine pictures to show just now, & he wishes you would give him a look in. The last I saw of his (in Watts's studio some time ago)—a landscape with soldiers—struck me as a most noble work, far more complete than such things of his used to be. I wish you would go & see his present works. I believe they would greatly please you, from all I hear. You probably know that his present address is 41 Addison Gardens North.[2]

Thanks about the chalk heads. I will bear what you say in mind whenever I have anything by me which seems suitable for the exchange.

Ever yours

D G Rossetti

60

P. S. I should have explained that I made the replica 2 inches less in height as there seemed perhaps more space than needed in yours.

LETTER 74

Kelmscott   3rd April 1874
Lechlade

My dear Leyland

I have only just got your note of 31st March on my return here. I went up for the wedding,[1] but was far from well while in London & understood you were not in town. Were it not that I am still the victim of a horrid cold & sore throat which are not likely to have left me by Sunday, I should be very glad to see you then; but as it is, a more opportune moment might probably turn up in better weather & when the Roman Widow picture might be as I should like to show it, which is not the case at present.[2] The dress being *drapery* & not *costume*, it takes (like the Proserpine) a great deal of study & alteration. It will however be fully equal to any picture of mine & I trust even to make it, when complete, my usual one step forward. It is occupying me entirely & I should now be obliged to you for a second £200 cheque on its account. I have no doubt if you could find a moment to run down in a month's time I should then be glad to show it.

I have also made a chalk drawing from Miss W. (subject— "Madonna Pietra" from Dante)[3]—with a view to your fourth picture if it suits you. It will be about the size of the "Proserpine" but perhaps a little wider—would hang however excellently with that. A pen & ink sketch of the whole arrangement would best give an idea of it, so I will make one & let you see it.

Ever yours

D G Rossetti

I went to see Hunt's picture. If the dealers offer it you at a small profit on the cost price of 10,000£, I should say on the whole, Dont buy.[4]

P S About that *Madonna Pietra* subject I named to you, I came to conclusion that it might suit you well as to size if I make it a sitting instead of a standing figure. Will show you the drawing when you come.

Speke Hall
^{n} Liverpool
10th Ap^l 1874

My dear Rossetti,

I enclose cheque for £200 on account of the picture of the Roman Widow—thus leaving £188 for payment on its completion.

The second picture you have to paint is one the size of Veronica or the Roman Widow and I should prefer a picture of this size rather than that of the Proserpine which I find a difficult size to hang advantageously.

I hope to be able to run down to see you for an hour or two some Sunday later on.

Yours truly

Fred. R. Leyland

D. G. Rossetti Esq

Kelmscott   April 11
Lechlade   1874

My dear Leyland

I shall be delighted to see you here before long at some propitious moment & show you the picture.

Thanks for cheque £200 to hand. My memoranda make the residue *190*-13-4. Is this incorrect?

I judge that I am now free to offer the *Madonna Pietra* subject elsewhere.

Ever yours

D G Rossetti

F R Leyland Esq

LETTER 77

Speke Hall
n Liverpool
15 Apl 1874

My dear Rossetti,
I make the balance of Roman Widow £188—thus—

cost----------£840-

debt of £1050 divided

Proserpine	£294
Roman Widow	252
similar picture	252
La Pia—	252
1050	---- £252

26 Dec cash 200
10 Apl adv   200   652

£188

Of course you are at liberty so far as I am concerned to offer Madonna Pietra elsewhere but I think on completion of the Roman Widow you ought to commence at once the similar sized picture you have engaged to paint; and indeed I quite understood that our agreement was that the work arranged for should be gone on with forthwith. When do you propose to take up La Pia? I am anxious to get the pictures finished in time for my new house next season if possible.

Yours truly

Fred R. Leyland

LETTER 78

Kelmscott   29 May 1874
Lechlade

My dear Leyland

I have been meaning to write you about the picture, & am eager to show it you, for I hope you will like it. But it is so nearly done that it seems a pity now for you to see it till quite finished; & this consummation is unluckily delayed by the non-appearance as yet of suitable roses. My own garden here failing me, I sent to some rose growers at Reading, but the specimens they send from my descrip-

63

tion do not answer, & there is nothing for it but to wait. Moreover there are wild roses needed too, & these no rose grower could supply in any case except the grower of all roses whoever he may be.

As soon as these are done I shall hope to be asking you to pay me a visit. I am just as anxious to see this final addition to the picture as you can be, for it will complete the scheme of whites throughout, I hope delightfully.

By the bye, if roses are desirable things, so are oranges. When you are quite bowed down by the weight of them, please shift some on to my shoulders here.

Ever yours

D G Rossetti

LETTER 79

Kelmscott   31 May [1874]
Lechlade

My dear Leyland

I see by adv^t that you are selling that large Leighton (& I suppose others—is the Turner yours?) at Christie's on 13th.[1] Would you mind sending in as yours that little Lucrezia, about which I have never seen at all as yet & which is still here? If so, I could forward it in your name to the Auctioneers, putting a reserved price of £100. An early—very early—& very quaint thing of mine, painted at 21, was bought by Agnew the other day at Christie's for nearly 400£ in Heugh's sale,[2] so it might perhaps answer to send this little drawing.

Ever yours

D G Rossetti

Of course it is needless to say that I do not propose your resuming possession of the thing, but merely fathering it at the sale.

LETTER 80

Kelmscott
Lechlade

13 June
1874

My dear Leyland

It seems that eternal Borgia thing is not in the sale after all. I don't want to bother you, but should let you know, as you told me you wrote Christies about it. Can you explain?[1]

The roses of the kind I want still rather hang fire here, so the picture follows suit. Would some time next week or the one following suit you to look up here? I would try for Brown to meet you, as he told me you had proposed coming in his company.[2]

But first I must get the picture thoroughly fit for showing you, & of course feel more nervous about it the nearer it gets to a finish.

Ever yours

D G R

LETTER 81

Kelmscott
Lechlade

19 June
1874

My dear Leyland

The muddle at Christies is incomprehensible to me. The thing was sent in plenty of time & I sent you a copy of the letter which went with it from here. Had you mentioned *my* name to them as the sender? If so, I did not know it; but even if so, they should have seen by the tone of the letter that it was identical with *my* sending it in your name.

Would you now kindly send me *by return* an order on Christies for withdrawing the picture, as it has been spoken of *as yours* all along; otherwise I have reason to believe they will be putting it into some other sale which might not suit me. I would then get Howell to see to it.

I write to London also, as I don't know your whereabouts.

Will hope to see you & show you the picture on 11th July.

Ever yours

D G Rossetti

Pardon all this bother in this bungled affair.

I heard of Whistler's Ex^n & wished him luck.[1]

LETTER 82

22 June
1874

My dear Leyland

Thanks for the order.

I am heartily pleased that you are convinced of my Proserpine being, as I told you it was, my best picture. I suppose one must always reckon that extraneous testimony is needed to establish a fact of the kind; though it is so long before work of my own satisfies me at all that I have learned to balance its claims exactly & correctly. I hope the Lilith hangs opposite now. If so, it with the *Di's Manibus* will make up a quartet I shall not be ashamed of as things go. This last gains enormously in colour now the roses are painted. It will never quite equal the Proserpine with the highest judgments, because of its lacking the sublimity of type which appears in that: but in point of pictorial advance, I have certainly never done a better thing.

Ned Jones's favour to my work is very very precious to me. I had already had just lately from Sandys a letter of generous—too generous—rapture on the picture of Proserpine. And now that you really like it, I may go on my way fully encouraged. It will make our meeting in July all the more welcome to me to know that you believe I have done my best for you: and I hope the picture I then show you may produce a like impression. Perhaps I may get a drawing or two for the other one ready besides. I have more than one subject in my head.

Ever yours D G R

P.S. By the bye, WHAT a haul you did make with that blessed Leighton, the frame did it![1] You must feel rather tempted to give up buying other pictures to keep, & buy nothing but Leightons to sell.

LETTER 83

23 Queens Gate
10 July 1874

My dear Rossetti,

I enclose cheque for £188 to complete purchase of Dis Manibus.
Pray send an acknowledgement of its receipt to Liverpool.
I start for Kelmscott tomorrow by the 2.15 train.

Yours truly

Fred R. Leyland

LETTER 84

17 Aug [1874]
16 Cheyne Walk

My dear Leyland

You will, either soon or later, be receiving the bill for the frame of
the Dïs Manibus picture. As I have not charged frames in cases
where the pictures have taken me less time, I think it best to mention this, & meant to do so before, but forgot it always. I have usually charged Graham the frames for his pictures.

Trusting to see you when again in town.

I am yours always

D G Rossetti

LETTER 85

Chelsea

12 Dec: 1874

My dear Leyland

Since seeing you I have been very hard at work on the picture of
La Bella Mano[1]—girl washing her hands with 2 attendant Cupids—
for which you saw drawing & rough design. It will be the *very best of
its kind* I have done—the head hair neck & shoulders being now quite
finished & *much superior* in quality to the Veronica which I have kept
by me while painting. It is more luminous & better in every way.
As I wish it to be yours if you like, I now write you word about it

—my reason being that I think you w^d be very sorry to miss it; otherwise nothing I could do would be surer of sale elsewhere, so I do not in the least wish to press you about it if you are disinclined. It would be precisely suited for one side of the fireplace, & then I could paint you a companion picture. The price (if sold *now*) I w^d fix at 1000 guineas. Its size is 58 X 46, & it has 3 figures. The Veronica is 42-33.

I particularly wish for an answer by Monday morning if possible; as some one is likely to come in on Monday who w^d probably snap up the picture if then unsold. But I give you the first offer.

Ever yours

D G Rossetti

I name above the full size of the present canvas. It is even possible that I may have to get it lined & a little enlarged, but I hope to avoid this.[2]

LETTER 86

19 Feb: 1875

16 Cheyne Walk

My dear Leyland

I ought to keep you informed that I got from Queen Square[1] two further variations of the paper, much inferior however to the first. On comparing the first with my own pattern, I think it may be made to do if a lighter fibre is introduced in the leaves of the dark branch —that part of the pattern being rather cutting, though much less so here than in the later versions.[2]

I am returning all to Wardle[3] today. If you wish now to give an order for any quantity (with my last revision) it is ready as far as I am concerned.

Ever yours

D G Rossetti

LETTER 87

16 Cheyne Walk
16 July 1875

My dear Leyland

I sent to you yesterday a sample paper which I have at last got for you out of Morris & Co. but I don't know whether your plans are quite changed on the point or not. The paper seems to me very good now except that it still tends a little rather to green than grey. Nevertheless I am not certain whether making it greyer might not possibly result in coldness.

I reckoned on sending you with this letter a pen-&-ink sketch I made with a view to the outstanding commission for you, same size as Veronica. However the making of the sketch yesterday only results in my finding it not to be interesting enough. I have a fresh version of the *Madonna Pietra* in my head & may probably be sketching that forthwith (or something else) & sending it on unless I see you. I lately got into the *La Pia* & was utterly dismayed to find on close examination that it has begun to crack in the 7 years or so since it was painted. The ground was different from any other picture of mine, & to that the lamentable accident is evidently attributable, as its nature shows. I am sure no other picture of mine would go in the same way, & never saw the least tendency of the sort before in one. This however rendered it impracticable to go on with the picture, & I must either commence a replica (an uncertain experiment always) or else substitute another work for your commission, which I remember is a plan you always expressed yourself willing to adopt.

As regards the *Venus Astarte* and the *Pandora*, which have been in question between us in an indeterminate way, I trust to be getting at the former as soon as I am in the country again, & about the latter with no great delay. I do not know if you retain your wish to possess them, and of course do not consider you pledged to them, as no price has ever been mentioned. This would be £2000 g^s apiece. The size of the *Astarte* (which I am cartooning) is 73 X 42 inches. The other w^d I suppose be about the same or a little taller.[1]

Ever yours   D G Rossetti

LETTER 88

Tuesday
20 July [1875]

My dear Leyland

Will you kindly send the sample paper back to 26 Queen Square, as I don't know whether they may be needing it. I will myself write a line to Wardle.

I will be sending you very shortly a sketch as suggestion for next picture.

I wish it might still prove somehow possible for the two works to be yours in which you have all along shown so much interest; but it would have been quite impracticable to paint them at any price resembling the other pictures you have of mine. Indeed the Proserpine should in reality have been more highly priced, but for my anxiety at the time to furnish you with a picture towards our engagements after long delay. Between ideal subjects of that kind & all others there is a gulf fixed as to labour & effort.

Ever yours

D G Rossetti

LETTER 89

16 Cheyne Walk, Chelsea
18 Aug 1875

My dear Leyland

I am beginning a picture[1] as companion to the "Veronica,"—indeed the head and shoulders as well as the arms and hands are nearly finished. It is as brilliant in painting as anything I have done or can do. I may perhaps quote to it the lines of Coleridge:—
"A damsel with a dulcimer
In a vision once I saw:
It was an Abyssinian maid,
And on her dulcimer she played,
Singing of Mount Abora."[2]

It represents the lady (Miss W.) seated by a tree on which her instrument is hung, and playing on it in an attitude of passionate absorption, while her hair spreads wide over the bough above her, and a dove seated in the tree stretches its neck low along a branch with its wings raised, and hearkens to the magic lay. Thus here the bird listens to the player, as in the other picture the player listens to the bird. I would send you a pen-&-ink sketch, but am so busy that I do not like to stop & make one, & am dead sure of the picture pleasing you. It progresses fully as fast as the "Veronica" did.

I wish you could have had the "Venus Astarte," and should have felt pleasure in knowing that it hung with my other pictures on your walls: but as I could only by any possibility paint so important an ideal subject in one way, i.e. thoroughly, & its size also being considered—it was impossible to do so for less than the 2000 guineas, which prevented me from answering your letter at the time. This sum I have since engaged it for to a new buyer, a friend of Howell's, whom he introduced to me.

Ever yours

D G Rossetti

F R Leyland Esq[3]

LETTER 90

23 Aug 1875

16 Cheyne Walk
Chelsea

My dear Leyland

As I am not likely to see you for more than a week, and as the whole of the figure is now in on the canvas from nature, I would be obliged if you would send me £200 by return, since I wish to stick to it & go ahead with the picture.

Ever yours

D G Rossetti

F R Leyland Esq

LETTER 91

16 Cheyne Walk
25 Aug 1875

My dear Leyland

Thanks for cheque £200 on acc^t of the new picture in hand for you.

Ever yours

D G Rossetti

LETTER 92

20 Sept 1875

My dear Leyland

Please send me by return £200 on further account of the picture in hand. It is in a most forward state—indeed would doubtless be finished now if there had not been an endless delay in getting a sea-gull set up by a naturalist in the position in which I need to paint him. This bird I am now promised at last tomorrow, & besides this there are only very minor details to add—the whole only a little time to spend further. The picture is completely successful[1] —the head now quite as beautiful as any I have done from the model—the drapery perhaps the best I have yet painted. I have introduced flowers—a wreath of autumn anemones round the head —a growth of antirrhinum at the base of the picture—&c. I shall be glad to show it you when you turn up; though perhaps it might be pleasantest to do so now when finished, as this will so soon be the case.

Ever yours

D G Rossetti

P.S. I am sure you will be concerned to hear that poor Graham has now actually lost his second son.[2]

LETTER 93

Thursday
23 Sept 1875

My dear Leyland

Did you get my note a few days ago requesting you to remit £200 on further account of the picture, & giving you an account of its progress? It is getting towards a completion, and I would be obliged by your remitting the £200 by return, as I happen to need it.

Ever yours

D G Rossetti

LETTER 94

Friday [24 September 1875?]

My dear Leyland

Thanks for cheque £200 on further acc^t of the picture.

Ever yours

D G Rossetti

LETTER 95

16 Cheyne Walk
6th Oct 1875

My dear Leyland

I may probably be leaving town early next week for the seaside—at last!—how long to stay I don't exactly know. Being asked for references by the landlady of a house near Bognor, I bethought me of you as one who would perhaps give me your good word as a tenant for her house if she writes. Would you kindly do so?

The picture is now substantially finished. A few days more work will have it complete before I go, save for a little possible last glazing which had better be left till my return when the surface w^d be quite dry. I w^d be obliged if, in answer to this, you w^d send me the remainder of its price—I suppose about 190£, but I dare say you can tell exactly.

The picture is, I hope & believe, the most brilliant piece of light & colour I have ever painted. It is now full of material, after my usual fashion. I suppose there is hardly a chance of showing it you within the next few days.

Ever yours

D G Rossetti

LETTER 96

16 C[heyne] W[alk]
Wednesday [6 October 1875]

My dear Leyland

I have just posted one note, & now remember that a question was omitted.

Do you wish the new picture framed in conformity with the present frame of the Veronica, or do you wish new frames for both, similar to the Roman Widow?

Ever yours

DGR

LETTER 97

Speke Hall
^{n} Liverpool
8 Oct 1875

My dear Rossetti,

I enclose cheque for £188 in payment of the remainder of the cost price of the companion picture to Veronica. The payments have been as follows

part of old debt	---------------	£252
24 Aug 1875	---------------	200
23 Sept	---------------	200
8 Oct	---------------	<u>188</u>
		<u>840</u>

I shall be up in town early next week—probably Wednesday—and I hope to see you before you leave town. If I should miss seeing you I think you had better send all the pictures to 49 Princes Gate—they will be safer there than at Cheyne Walk during your absence. Moreover I expect to get into the house in about six weeks or two months.

I have not heard from the landlady of the house you propose taking. I will write to her immediately I have any enquiry from her.

Yours truly

Fred R. Leyland

By the bye—will you send me the sight measure of this picture also that of the Roman Widow. What do you intend to christen the companion to Veronica.

LETTER 98

16 Cheyne Walk
Chelsea
9 Oct 1875

My dear Leyland

It is probable I may be making a move about Wednesday, but if you w^d certainly be here & able to dine with me that day (Wed^y) I would wait till then for certain. Please let me know. Perhaps you could look in by daylight & come later to dinner or stay on between-whiles. I fancy the pictures would remain quite as safely here as elsewhere unless you wish otherwise. The new one may need last looking at & last touches on my return to town. I propose to call it "The Song of Mount Abora" & to inscribe the quotation on frame. This picture is 36 X 43 inches. The Veronica is 34 1/2 X 43. The Roman Widow is 36 1/2 X 41. I give *size* measures—*sight* w^d be a trifle less.

I perceive the new picture should hang with the Roman Widow—not with the other. The drapery is white in both—I had to reject the gold stuff which was too heavy, & it goes much better with R. W. than with V. only the frames don't match as the others do.

Ever yours

D G Rossetti

LETTER 99

Monday [11 October 1875]

My dear Leyland

At 12 on Wed^y or later I shall be happy to see you. At any earlier hour the picture would be happy to be seen. If the two can be combined, welcome.

I shall not be leaving on Wed^y but a day or two later.

Ever yours

D G Rossetti

The picture will still be lacking some last details when you see it.

LETTER 100

Speke Hall
n Liverpool
5 April 1876

My dear Rossetti,
I have to be in my new house in a fortnight from this so I will be glad if you will send in at once my pictures so that I may get them hung. I don't know whether you have yet finished the last picture; but if not you had better retain it at Cheyne Walk.

Yours truly

Fred. R. Leyland

When do you come back to town?—

LETTER 101

Aldwick Lodge
Bognor
9 April [1876]

My dear Leyland

I am writing with this to Dunn to send your 4 pictures[1] to Prince's Gate—don't know the number but of course it will be easily found. The fifth—last done—needs little work—only strings to instrument

& some glazing. This I will do as soon as possible on my return which will be very shortly.

I shall have several botherations to attend to on my return, having been away so long; & shall not be seeing any one just now. It will give me pleasure to have a quiet look in from you as heretofore a little later, if you have a spare moment for one so little worth interviewing.

With kind regards

Yours ever

D G Rossetti

LETTER 102

Tuesday [25 July 1876?]
Chelsea

My dear Leyland

I thought to see you Sunday evening & meant then to have said what I now write.

I have been so seedy that I have seen no one, & consequently no one has seen that finished head (La Ricordanza)[1] which I think pleased you as much as anything I have done, & I feel sure I never did a better thing.

My price for it is £500. I don't want to be looking up others[2] & w^d be glad if you would buy it, as I will not disguise from you that I am somewhat short of funds, & your manner when we met was so grateful to me in its affection that I may speak frankly.

If it did not suit you to buy the picture, would you oblige me by advancing by return £300 on its security—the sum to be repaid on my sale of it which cannot be long delayed.

Sincerely yours D G Rossetti

P S Perhaps, as you did not see Watts (who was here Sunday evening) your best plan might be to write him a line (W. T. Watts 3 Putney Hill) respecting the M. S. matter. He will willingly enter into it.

LETTER 103

Liverpool
26th July 1876

My dear Rossetti,
The picture La Ricordanza will not suit me owing to its size:—
when you see my drawing room you will find I am limited by the
scheme of decoration to half lengths like Veronica.

I will however lend you the £300 you ask for with pleasure until
you sell the picture and I now enclose cheque for that amount.

I go up to town this morning and will probably see you tonight;
but send me an acknowledgement for the money here all the same.

Yours ever

Fred R Leyland

D. G. Rossetti Esq
16 Cheyne Walk
Chelsea
S W

LETTER 104

Chelsea
27 July 1876

My dear Leyland

Many thanks for cheque £300 safely received as an advance to
be repaid on my sale of the picture La Ricordanza.

Yours sincerely

D G Rossetti

F R Leyland Esq

LETTER 105

19 March [1877]

My dear Leyland

I will see about lining the picture forthwith. I am a little foggy as to
our relations to it. When enlarged to an 800 guinea picture,[1] does

78

it fall in with the old commissions or rank as a new one? My notes have got rather confused.

I should mention that, having framed the picture once on its present scale, I should have to transfer the cost of the new frame to you. Indeed, except in the case of the Astarte, the price of which was a high one, I have lately charged frames to the purchasers.

I don't know whether you are a Londoner or Liverpoolian this week. If the former, try & look in & dine with me one day. I have a cook who cooks a good dinner & would even make a good picture!

Ever yours

D G Rossetti

Of course I remember that there is in any case an advance of 300£ on the present picture.

LETTER 106

Liverpool
27 Mar: 1877

My dear Rossetti,
   I merely write to put on record that the commission for Astarte[1] is a new one—and quite independent of the old outstanding one—of La Pia—and that the price is to be £840 and that I have to pay for the frame.

Yours ever

Fred R Leyland

LETTER 107

28 March [1877]

My dear Leyland

Thanks for your specification. The picture is gone to the liner's, & will arise like a phoenix from its ashes before long.

Some sluggishness seems to weigh on the proposed *Sea–Spell* Sonnet, which I must manage to dissipate. Were inspiration to awake in my mind in this direction, my late clairvoyant experiences[1] seem to point to a probability that an ardour would simultaneously arise in your mind to settle for the frame so decorated with Ford & Dickinson. Is not this even so? You know this frame matches the Veronica one, & both flank the new lengthened picture *à merveille*.

Ever yours

D G Rossetti

LETTER 108

Monday [April 1877]

My dear Leyland

The frame-makers have been written to to send the tablet to-night if done, as I suppose it is, & in that case the sonnet[1] will be inscribed on it tomorrow, & it will reach your house either Wednesday or Thursday. Thus I doubt not it will be in its place when you reach town again, & I hope will thoroughly please you by its effect on your walls.

Tomorrow Miss Wilding comes to sit for the shoulders & arms of the Hero, so I hope to have made some way with that picture when I see you again which I trust to do about close of the week.

Ever yours

D G Rossetti

LETTER 109

16 May 1877

My dear Leyland

Would you oblige me by sending cheque £300 on further account of the Hero which is now far advanced, & I believe quite successful.

Ever yours

D G Rossetti

LETTER 110

18 May 1877

My dear Leyland

Thanks for cheque £300 on further account of the *Hero* picture, making now £600 paid on it.

I shall be glad of a look in from you on Sunday as you were suggesting. No doubt you w^d [be] either alone or with a lady. The Hero is not sufficiently advanced yet to show up with complete effect, & the studio is otherwise quite unprovided for a display of work.

I have been very seedy for some days, & fear I must have been but dull company last night, which I knew you would pardon.

Ever yours

D G Rossetti

LETTER 111

Woolton Hall[1]
^{n} Liverpool
31 July 1877

My dear Rossetti,
I enclose you cheque for £500 on account of pictures which is to be appropriated as follows—
In completion of payment for Hero £240—say

paid 26 July 1876—	300
17 May 1877	300
now	240
	840

and £260 on account of La Pia or the other picture to be painted instead of it. This makes £512 paid on La Pia—say

part of old debt £252	
now	260
	512

Pray let me know you receive it safely and how it is placed.

Yours truly

Fred. R. Leyland

D G Rossetti Esq

LETTER 112

My dear Leyland

What an age it is since I have seen you, & how long it was before I thought to be able to write again to my friends! Not till just now am I beginning to venture to announce myself well again, up to which announcement, all tidings of me w^d have been worse than nothing. It is time now to tell you that I have returned to London for more than a month & am in good working order again.[1] My long neglect of writing to you has been enforced on me this very evening by the first chance I have had of getting to the background of the *Hero* picture. This chance is a bloom of magnolia, kindly sought for at my request & sent up by Mrs Cowper Temple. This I want to make helpful in the *Hero* picture; & shall try tomorrow, though it *may* not turn out the thing after all.

It was not till my return to London that I saw the note you had written me touching the disposal in work of the £500 I had from you. Would it suit you that, beyond the balance on the *Hero*, I should defray the rest by a separate work,—either a £280 picture, or else a portrait of yourself or some member of your family? I w^d try & do my best for it in either case, & was never well enough at that time to thank you properly for the helping hand you lent me.

Will you remember me most kindly to Mrs Leyland and all your family circle. I should have written earlier since my return, had I not thought it possible that a flying visit to town might bring the aroma of your cigarette & your friendly greeting through my darkling studio doorway as of old.

With best Xmas & New Year's wishes,

I am ever

sincerely yours

D G Rossetti

LETTER 113

Thursday [1878?]

My dear Leyland

That was random talk of mine the other day about exhibiting.[1] I do not know what my plans are, & have spoken to absolutely no one but yourself, so please do not say a word to *anyone*. Of course this needs no answer.

Ever yours   D G Rossetti

LETTER 114

Friday [late 1870's?]

My dear Leyland

I told the poor fellow (Cartledge)[1] of whom I spoke to you to write you a line & now hear he has done so. I hope you may think it possible to give him a place of some sort. Anything would be a boon, & you wd be doing a good deed.

I got the 2 pictures from Prince's Gate. Hoping soon to see you.

Ever yours   D G Rossetti

LETTER 115

Woolton Hall
n Liverpool
14 Apl 1879

Dear Gabriel,

I am coming up to town for the season the end of next week. Will you return the pictures you have of mine before then. Are you going to make any alteration to the knees of the figure in the "Sea-Spell"?

I have looked at my memorandum of the payments on account of "Hero" and "La Pia" and find they are as follows

```
         Hero—price  £840

26 July 1876   cash  £300
17 May 1877    adv   300
31 July 1877   adv   240
(remer of 500—part
to Hero—remainder
to La Pia)               ____
                         £840


     La Pia price   £840
part of debt of £1050
divided according to
your letters in October
& November 1873 —    £252
31 July 1877—cash—
as above—             260
                      512
leaving—still to pay  328
                      840
```

Yours truly

Fred. R. Leyland

LETTER 116

Woolton Hall
n Liverpool
3 March 1880

My dear Gabriel,

I have received a sad blow. My dear daughter[1] died yesterday in childbirth, and I am completely broken hearted.

Afftly yours

Fred R Leyland

LETTER 117

Woolton Hall
Liverpool
14 March 1880

My dear Gabriel,

It was a great comfort to me to receive your kind letter. Everything in life seemed so dull and hopeless that the sympathy of so old a friend was most welcome.

I fear it will be some time before I get over the shock so sudden and unsuspected a blow has been to me. I am trying to get up to town next week, for this place, with the memory of my dear child so fresh and vivid, is distressing to all of us.

Yours

Fred R. Leyland

LETTER 118

Sunday [30 May 1880]

My dear Leyland

I really found it so difficult to deal with your very reasonable urgency today, that it will be best just to write a line about it.

There are of course stages of work in the midst of which one cannot knock off. I am in such a one with my present picture in hand,[1] but when that gets a respite in about a month, hope for certain to take in hand simultaneously some of your work & Graham's.

Pardon my troubling you with M S on the subject, but a line will sometimes avoid cross-purposes in conversation.

Ever yours

D G Rossetti

LETTER 119

[49, Prince's Gate, S. W.
10 June 1880

My dear Gabriel,

I have been trying to make up my mind to buy your picture[1] but I really cannot.

I have put so much money in pictures already that I do not care to put any more; and I shall fill up the new room with pictures from the office.

Did you see the account in Tuesday's Times of the sale at Christies and the tremendous fall in the value of pictures—as much as fifty or sixty percent.

Rather a bad look out for collectors.[2]

Yours [illegible]

Fred R Leyland]

LETTER 120

3 Oct/ 80

My dear Leyland

Since last seeing you I have been exclusively at work on the La Pia picture which is now very far towards completion. Would you kindly send me £150 on account of the balance, which I believe is £328.

Yours ever

D G Rossetti

P S I expect the picture to be ready for delivery in quite a few weeks.

LETTER 121

Woolton Hall
n Liverpool
11 Oct 1880

My dear Gabriel,

I have been at Boulogne for the last three weeks and only got your letter on my return today. I enclose you a cheque for £150 on account of "La Pia" picture and am glad to hear you are getting on so quickly with it.— I was only a day in London when I passed through or I would have called to see you.

When are you going on with the Hero picture? You don't seem to me to be entirely satisfied with it and I fear it is not a labour of love to you. What do you think of letting me have the Blessed Damoiselle instead. I would be willing to pay you something more; but consider you have already had £840. I suggest this as I really want a picture at once to finish my drawing room and this and La Pia will fill up all the wall space I have left. If the thing doesn't suit you don't hesitate to say so frankly and make the best you can of the picture as it is.

Yours [illegible]

Fred R Leyland

LETTER 122

Monday [18 October 1880?]

My dear Leyland

I append receipt.

I should have answered your former note earlier, but did not see my way to the proposal, of which perhaps you may speak, if you like to do so, when we meet.

I have now laid La Pia aside for a few days, but shall be resuming it immediately with, I trust, a fresh eye for some difficulties in the background paint which have caused me already to repaint it several times. It will then doubtless proceed rapidly to a finish; & in finishing I shall require the frame. Do you like me to order this for you from Ford & Dickinson, who are the only people whose work gives one satisfaction?

Yours sincerely

D G Rossetti

LETTER 123

28 Oct [1880]

My dear Leyland

I have ordered the frame for La Pia. I have now settled arrangement of background, but may probably have to put the picture by for finishing till I get the frame as a guide in tone. Then it will get rapidly out of hand.

Ever yours

D G Rossetti

LETTER 124

Woolton Hall
n Liverpool
14 Dec 1880

My dear Gabriel,
   Enclosed I send your cheque for £178 being completion of price for "La Pia"—

Yours [illegible]

Fred R Leyland

LETTER 125

Friday [17 December 1880?]

My dear Leyland

This is to acknowledge amended cheque £170 completing payment of *La Pia*. I have altered frame for *Mnemosyne*. This, when finished, will look as vigorous as any, & the head is of my very best.

Ever yours   D G Rossetti

LETTER 126

49, Prince's Gate, S. W.
31 Jany 1881

My dear Gabriel,
   I send you a cheque for £500 in payment for the "Blessed Damoiselle." Let me have a receipt that I may send down to the office.

I should like you to go on at once with what has to be done to the picture and to La Pia so that I may have them home.

Yours ever

Fred R Leyland

LETTER 127

49, Prince's Gate, S. W.
12 Ap^l 1881

My dear Gabriel,

I enclose cheque for £300 on account of the Beatrice[1] I have bought from you for 650 g^{nas}. Let me have a pleasant surprize and see it well on when I return from Venice.

Yours ever

Fred R Leyland

LETTER 128

49, Prince's Gate, S. W.
12 July 1881

My dear Gabriel,

I am sorry I could not call on you last Sunday but I will do so next.

The Blessed Damoiselle is placed and looks superb. The light suits it admirably and if you could only see it you would be pleased.

I want you to finish the glazing of La Pia and let me have it before I go away.

The Blessed Damoiselle occupies one wall of the portico room; the Eve of St Agnes another and the remaining one is waiting for La Pia. Do, like a good fellow, finish it and let it go.

Yours ever

Fred R Leyland

LETTER 129

My dear Leyland

In writing last, I meant to have asked you whether you could now lend me the *Sea–Spell* for a month or so, as I ought now to be doing the reduced replica for which you gave permission.[1] If so, I wd send Ford & Dickinson about it—all expenses of course being mine.

Ever yours

D G Rossetti

LETTER 130

3rd Sept [1881]

My dear Leyland

I just got a telegram from Liverpool to say that the large picture there is sold.[1] I ought as soon as possible to commence replica of *Sea–Spell*. Wd you kindly send an order that I can forward to Ford & Dickinson or Vacani[2] to remove it here, or if you prefer perhaps you will write them a line direct.

I cannot get the Salutation frame out of F. & D. though I keep besieging them with post cards.

Yours ever

D G Rossetti

LETTER 131

Wednesday [7 September 1881]

My dear Leyland

The frame for the *Salutation* arrived yesterday & looks wonderfully well.

Did you get my last note? But perhaps you are away. I should much like to get promised loan of the Sea–Spell as soon as you can kindly manage it.

Yours ever

D G Rossetti

LETTER 132

Woolton Hall
n Liverpool
12 Sept 1881

My dear Gabriel,

I enclose cheque for £200 on further acct of picture of the Salutation.

Yours

Fred R Leyland

LETTER 133

Monday [autumn 1881]

My dear Leyland

I find there was a flattering unction in my view of the balance on the *Salutation*. It is altogether £232-10. Would you kindly send me this, and the picture will be the first I finish & deliver. I have got to work on it today.

Ever yours

D G Rossetti

LETTER 134

[autumn 1881]

My dear Leyland

You may probably remember that before painting your "Salutation", I had begun it on a rather smaller scale. This beginning, Dunn[1] has carried on now as regards the first laying in, and has forwarded it here with the original (most safely packed) for me to work on if it becomes possible, which is not the case at present.

I meant to have explained this to you by letter, when first the idea of doing it struck me, but my weakness made it go by. Meanwhile pray believe that your picture is in perfect safety. I think that your friendship will raise no objection[2] to my carrying out the first smaller version if feasible, as it would always remain quite secondary to yours.

I am still expecting the oranges about which you kindly telegraphed.

Yours ever

D G Rossetti

LETTER 135

Thursday [winter 1881-82]

My dear Leyland

I will take care to get the pictures sent you in the early part of next week.

I have altered the knees in Sea—Spell which is a great improvement: also lessened the portion of back showing beyond the shoulder, which seemed perhaps incompatible with the amount of bosom seen.

I shall have to borrow this picture again when you return to Woolton, on account of the reduction I have in hand.

Thanks for particulars as to commissions. It will be very pleasant to see you again when in town, though I fancy you voted me rather a shady lot last time.

Ever yours

D G Rossetti

LETTER 136

49, Prince's Gate, S. W.
31 Jany 1882

My dear Gabriel,

I find the absence of the Sea—Spell leaves such an unpleasant vacant space on the walls, that I cannot let it go. And I would prefer that Dunn copied it here so that he can replace the picture in the frame every evening.

Yours [illegible]

Fred R Leyland

LETTER 137

My dear Leyland

I was hoping, from what you wrote, to see you by end of last week. I hope you are not ill. I wish I could say that I am any better myself.

All your splendid oranges are exhausted, alas! When in town, I gave several doz: to my mother & William's little ones, thinking they wd not keep. If you could send me some more, I wd be more thrifty! They are divine and the only things I can enjoy.

Ever yours

D G Rossetti

Appendix

Included in this appendix are full or partial texts of four letters which Rossetti wrote to Leyland but which may or may not have been received.

LETTER A

[This fragment, which bears the notation "never sent" in Rossetti's hand, is probably the draft which Rossetti sent to Ford Madox Brown (L 1175), and can therefore be dated 30 May 1873.]

Kelmscott
Lechlade

My dear Leyland,

The chalks in which the drawing I sent is executed are hardly very "frail & perishable" though the label put on the back for safety's sake may seem alarming. Many rooms at the Louvre are full of such drawings—indeed much more powdery ones than this—which have been safe for a century & a half or nearly that; & no material perhaps is *so* safe if kept carefully; and numberless things of the kind by Gainsborough and others exist unhurt.

I need not hesitate to say that your letter is an anxious one to me. When last we entertained the subject of your commissions to me (rather more than a year ago,) your views were, to have 7 pictures—a large one & two smaller ones for the place over the piano in the back drawing room,—two of the smaller size to face these, & 2 similar ones to face my two in front drawing room. I had thought of substituting the Desdemona for the Dante subject (at a less price than the latter) but since you said that smaller pictures throughout would suit you better than this I had still supposed that the 7 originally projected would hold good, and that the *La Pia* would probably take the centre over the piano. You had so decidedly said that you wished the drawing-rooms to contain my work that I had not doubted the continuance of this plan, and had reckoned on it as the leading item of my work for some time to come, & as a matter to which I meant to do the fullest justice I could.

All I have done for you as yet has, I believe, given you complete satisfaction. The dissatisfied person has been myself at times; and I have lately given more than 2 months time to increasing the merit & value of 2 finished pictures—the Lilith & Loving Cup—and completing with my best efforts 2 others—the Blessed Damozel drawing & the little Lucrezia Borgia. Much of this work was what you would never have thought of claiming as due; you know me well enough to be sure that I found no exaggerated pretensions on it. At the same time I know you well enough also to be convinced that you will think some consideration due (apart from friendship) to the evidence of my doing my very best for your commissions, even after original completion or (I may say especially as regards the chalk drawing) beyond original intention.

I was not aware that I was owing you more than double the £500 due on the proposed Dante subject. Are you certain that no portion of the extra 550£ was liquidated on account of other work since delivered? I find myself 3 entries of cheques received from you amounting to this sum in all (& the only ones of whose destination I am uncertain at present,)—viz:—25th Aug 1868 £150 7th June 1869 200£ 9th June 1869 £200. Our transactions have been at such long intervals that I will ask you, who have probably kept exact memoranda, to tell me to what these entries refer.

It is unpleasant to be writing in [illegible], & all the more to a friend; but unluckily I have never got free of the necessity of living by the work of the moment, & therefore whatever I work on has to be drawn upon while in progress. I shall soon have made considerable progress with one of the pictures of which I spoke to you, & can then show it you; but if the little designs I send you should convince you of the certainty of the 2 pictures pleasing you (and without feeling such certainty, by experience of your tastes, I should not have offered them,) I would be glad now to receive the requested advance of 400£. They will then both proceed with no delay.

LETTER B

[This letter appears on L 1267, and is said to be based on a copy; no original appears among the LC letters.]

Kelmscott,
11th March, 1874

Dear Leyland,

Would the 4th picture (besides *La Pia*, *Proserpine* and *R. Widow*) suit you to match *Proserpine* or thereabouts in size? If so I have an excellent subject (fair) and would set about it.

Ever yours,
D. G. R.

LETTER C

[This pencilled fragment refers to the negotiations over *Mnemosyne* and *The Blessed Damozel*, and can therefore be assigned to the winter of 1880-81.]

P S You will remember that ab^t a year ago, you wished to gain [several words illegible], and you have since said that the one difficulty [several words illegible]. . . .

Considering the difficulty with the Memory picture, I w^d part with the B^d Dam^l to you for 500 guineas. You might have the Memory (when completed on present scale) into the bargain. I am much concerned that that picture has not resulted quite to my satisfaction (owing to the change of plan) but I feel that rather [several words illegible].

LETTER D

[This note is quoted by Val Prinsep in "A Collector's Correspondence" but no original appears in the LC collections. Its date makes it perhaps the last letter Rossetti ever wrote.]

Westcliff Bungalow, Birchington-on-Sea,
April 5th, 1882.

My dear Leyland,—

I find I am out of wine again. I do not know where to get the sort you so kindly sent me. It would be very kind of you to send me a little more to this address. I am feeling very weak to-day.

Notes to Letters

Letter 1

1. After 1862 Rossetti frequently used writing paper with an engraved design as a letterhead. This design included the address, "16 Cheyne Walk, Chelsea," and the motto "Frangas non Flectas." The use of [letterhead] in other letters indicates that this engraved paper was used. (Photograph Courtesy of the Library of Congress).

2. This letter is apparently the second letter Rossetti wrote to Leyland. Val Prinsep, in "A Collector's Correspondence" (*Art Journal*, 54 [1892], 250), refers to a letter dated 29 December 1865 in which Rossetti offered *Sibylla Palmifera*. This letter has apparently disappeared since then.

3. *Lady Lilith*, CR 205.

4. *Sibylla Palmifera*, CR 193, commissioned by George Rae.

Letter 3

1. Leyland evidently bought one of Smetham's drawings which he had seen in Rossetti's studio.

Letter 4

1. John Miller, Liverpool art dealer and sometime buyer, who first recommended Rossetti to Leyland.

2. *Heliogabalus, Emperor of Rome*, a watercolor based on this drawing, was exhibited by Simeon Solomon at the Dudley Gallery in 1868.

Letter 5

1. A portrait of Mrs. Leyland, *Monna Rosa*, CR 198.

2 Leyland kept Rossetti well supplied with oranges right up until Rossetti's death (see Letter 137, among others).

Letter 6

1. *The Loving Cup*, CR 201, was 26 X 18.

2. *A Christmas Carol*, CR 195; its size was 18 X 15 1/2. Ms. Surtees does not assign ownership to Leyland, but apparently he purchased it and then later exchanged it (see Letter 14).

3. Angelo Poliziano (1454-1494), Florentine poet.

4. "With a golden mantle, necklace, and rings, it pleases her to have with these nothing else but a rose in her hair."

5. Parts of this letter are quoted in Prinsep, "A Collector's Correspondence."

Letter 8

1. To Ford Madox Brown, 14 August: "All would be well as to the £10, were it not that I had to send that very sum to Lizzie's brother Harry, who has had the small-pox. . . . However, I suppose I must draw on Leyland on my account, and can then do the needful." (L 628)

2. Rossetti was going to vacation with William Allingham.

Letter 9

1. Speke Hall is a half-timbered manor house, built in the South Lancashire and Cheshire style during the period 1490-1612 by Sir William Norrys and his descendents. Its location just outside of Liverpool made it convenient to Leyland's shipping interests, and he leased Speke from 1866 to 1877. The property is now administered by the National Trust.

2. Louisa Jane Parke, governess for Leyland's daughters and an old acquaintance of Mrs. Gabriele Rossetti and Christina.

3. George Rae, one of Rossetti's chief buyers during this period.

4. Parts of this letter quoted in Prinsep, "A Collector's Correspondence."

Letter 10

1. Rossetti was now completing for Leyland a chalk study of *Venus Verticordia* (CR 173A).

2. At Rossetti's instigation Leyland had hired Murry Howell Murray the previous July. Howell's cousin proved to be a less than ideal employee and was discharged. Howell continued to be vexed by Murray: in the fall of 1871 he wrote to William Michael Rossetti that he had finally shipped his cousin off to Australia. See Helen Rossetti Angeli, *PreRaphaelite Twilight: The Story of Charles Augustus Howell* (London: Richards, 1954), pp. 23, 56.

Letter 12

1. Probably *Syracusan Bride Leading Wild Beasts to the Temple of Diana*, by Frederic Leighton (1830-1896), later sold by Leyland (see Letter 79).

2. *Lucrezia Borgia*, CR 124.

3. The B. G. Windus sale had taken place on 15 February.

Letter 13

1. Picture framers, often referred to as "F. & D."

Letter 14

1. John Marshall (1818-1891), anatomist and surgeon, Rossetti's usual physician and Brown's friend since their youth.

2. Probably *Sir Tristram and La Belle Yseult Drinking the Love Potion* (CR 200).

Letter 16

1. Perhaps CR 207A, since the head is from Mrs. Morris (see next letter), or another chalk drawing since lost.

2. *La Pia de' Tolomei*, CR 207. Rossetti worked on the painting until the early summer, then put it aside because it had not yet been sold (L 660). In August Leyland put £150 down on the picture, and added another £200 the following June, but despite these inducements the work was not completed until 1881.

Letter 17

1. William Graham (1816-1885), M. P. for Glasgow from 1865 to 1874. From this time forward he and Leyland were Rossetti's best patrons.

2. Rossetti had completed *Dante's Dream at the Time of the Death of Beatrice* (CR 81) as a small watercolour in 1856. By 1863 he had decided to undertake a large oil reproduction of it if he could secure a commission, and for this purpose the

photograph had been displayed. (The photograph itself had been made by the owner of the watercolour, Ellen Heaton, at the request of Ruskin.)

Graham offered Rossetti 1,500 guineas for the oil reproduction provided it did not exceed 3 1/2′ X 6′. When finished it was nearly 7′ X 12 1/2′ (CR 81.R.1) and Graham therefore refused it. The painting was eventually purchased by the Corporation of Liverpool.

3. CR 368, 369, 371, or perhaps 207A.

Letter 18

1. Rossetti, accompanied by Howell, had visited Leyland at Speke Hall from 3 August to 10 August. Speaking of their stay, Howell wrote to William Michael complaining of Rossetti's "total and absolute indifference to *every thing*." (Quoted in Angeli, *PreRaphaelite Twilight*, p. 63.)

2. Dr. Charles Bader (1827-1899), ophthalmic surgeon at Guy's Hospital.

3. Probably CR 207C.

4. CR 114.R.1. Leyland did not buy the painting.

Letter 19

1. Sir William Withey Gull (1816-1890), later physician-in-ordinary to the queen.

2. Dr. Möhrer.

3. The intention of undertaking a trip to Germany was very short-lived, because four days later Rossetti urges William Allingham to vacation with him: "We might go to several places even—say including a new visit to Stratford-on-Avon and neighbourhood, which will bear seeing often." (L 664).

4. A commission for an oil painting of *Aspecta Medusa* (CR 183), never completed.

5. Also a project which was never completed, perhaps never begun.

6. Probably *The Eve of St. Agnes*, exhibited at the Royal Academy in 1863.

7. Leyland's collection at the time of his death did not include any works by John Rogers Herbert (1810-1890).

Letter 21

1. A chalk drawing (CR 183E) for the proposed *Aspecta Medusa*.

Letter 22

1. *The Wine of Circe* by Sir Edward Burne-Jones, exhibited in 1869 at the Old Watercolour Gallery and bought by Leyland. Rossetti wrote a sonnet to accompany it.

2. This reference is puzzling, since no "Endymion & Diana" by G. F. Watts was ever exhibited at the Royal Academy. A painting entitled simply *Endymion* was shown by Watts but not until 1893. In 1869 Watts exhibited an *Orpheus and Eurydice* and perhaps this is the work Rossetti means; but in a letter to Alice Boyd describing his visit to the exhibition, Rossetti says that "Watts is not well represented." (L 704)

3. Probably *Three Girls*. Elizabeth and Joseph Pennell in their *Life of James McNeill Whistler* (Philadelphia: Lippincott, 1905), p. 108, date this failure as 1868. But Frederick Jameson, with whom Whistler was living at the time, places it in 1868 or 1869 (p. 103).

Letter 24

1. A proposed replica of *Sibylla Palmifera*, never completed (see Letter 30). To Alice Boyd: "I have accepted a distasteful but temptingly lucrative offer to make a replica in oil the same size . . . a very lazy leisurely job which can be done at odd times." (L 701-2) Doughty and Wahl erroneously assign this replica to Graham.

Letter 25

1. Leyland's son.

2. A reference to Howell's chicanery—cf. *Acts* V, 1-6.

Letter 26

1. Presumably Marie Spartali, daughter of the Greek consul-general, a gifted amateur painter and the model for *A Vision of Fiammetta* and other Rossetti paintings; see Letter 28.

Letter 27

1. Not catalogued in Surtees.

2. Whistler had been making several visits to Speke Hall to complete portraits of Leyland and his family.

3. Leyland's town residence was at 23 Queen's Gate, then (from 1876) at 49 Prince's Gate.

4. For several years Rossetti intended to paint an *Aspecta Medusa* for Leyland, and had even sold him a chalk drawing of the design (CR 183E) in 1867, but the work was never commissioned by Leyland.

Letter 30

1. Retitled *The Bower Meadow* (CR 229). The sketch described here (229B) was later abandoned and the finished oil shows considerable differences in composition.

2. *Beata Beatrix* (CR 168.R.3).

3. A new version of *Michael Scott's Wooing* (CR 222), commissioned by Leyland.

4. "The Stealthy School of Criticism," published in *The Athenaeum* on 16 December.

5. Parts of this letter are quoted in Prinsep, "A Collector's Correspondence."

Letter 31

1. CR 239. The work was at first accepted by Leyland and then refused; commissioned again by Graham in 1874 but later abandoned.

2. "Dante Alighieri to Guido Cavalcanti."

3. Guido and Lapo Gianni.

4. Lady Joan and Lady Lagia.

5. Dunn completed the work on this model—see Gale Pedrick, *Life with Rossetti, or No Peacocks Allowed* (London: Macdonald, 1964), p. 144.

6. Presumably a daughter or sister to Whistler's friend H. Gee—*Life of Whistler*, p. 135; a member of Leyland's "family circle" at Speke?

7. Parts of this letter quoted in Prinsep, "A Collector's Correspondence."

Letter 33

1. Parts of this letter quoted in Prinsep, "A Collector's Correspondence."

Letter 34

1. Rossetti to Brown, 10 February 1873: "Of course the *Loving Cup* story is all blundered. I did, about a year ago, get back Leyland's picture to work on it, and finding I didn't like it at all, proposed to take it back and allow for it in other work I was to do for him. Of course I meant to resume its ownership at original price, but have since had reason to suppose that Leyland means to charge me an advance (and a big one) according to my (supposed) present price for such a thing; ever since which discovery, I have meant to send him back the picture of course. . . . " (L 1135) See Letter 47.

2. *Dante's Dream.*

Letter 37

1. *Veronica Veronese*, CR 228, bought by Leyland at the price named. The model was Alexa Wilding.

2. Rossetti long cherished the idea of creating a large painting from his old pen-and-ink sketch of Cassandra (CR 127), but he never undertook it.

102

3. Parts of this letter quoted in Prinsep, "A Collector's Correspondence."

Letter 40

1. Altered version of this letter appears in L 1045-6.

Letter 44

1. To Brown: "I am having Leyland's *Lilith* sent here, as I think I can finish it from little May [Morris] who has the right complexion and I fear his getting out of temper if it doesn't reach him." (L 1088)

Letter 46

1. *Veronica Veronese.*

2. Henry Merritt (1822-1897), art restorer and critic for *The Standard.*

Letter 47

1. CR 254. Some drawings were made for this painting in 1874 and 1875, and a more earnest attempt was made between 1878 and 1881, but it was never completed.

2. *Ligea Siren* (CR 234). The model Rossetti described as "a singular housemaid of advanced ideas, known to Dunn." (L 1143).

3. Leyland owned Albert Moore's *Venus* (exhibited at the Royal Academy in 1869), *Sea Gulls,* and *Shells.*

4. Parts of this letter, erroneously dated 1872, appear in Prinsep, "A Collector's Correspondence."

Letter 49

1. To 200 guineas.

2. Unidentified. Possibly, since Howell was intimate with the Greek colony in London, the reference is to Christine Spartali, Marie's sister, who by marriage became Comtesse Edmond de Cahen.

3. Parts of this letter are quoted in Prinsep, "A Collector's Correspondence."

Letter 50

1. CR 244A.

2. *La Ghirlandata* (CR 232). Leyland balked at the three heads and Rossetti sold it to Graham.

3. From *The Times,* 18 April: "Public Schools Racquet Challenge Cup. The final match for the above was played yesterday at Prince's Club, Han's-place, between Harrow (P. F. Hadow and G. D. Leyland) and Rugby (J. Barrow and J. Harding). As anticipated, the Harrovians scored an easy win . . . at four games love in exactly half an hour."

Letter 51

1. An oil painting had been commissioned by Graham in 1871; it was begun again in 1873 based on this drawing, and completed in 1877.

Letter 52

1. To Ford Madox Brown, 30 May 1873: "Your surmises about Leyland were but too correct. . . . I may add, to relieve your mind, that I shall shortly be getting several hundreds from Parsons, so that this hitch with Leyland is not quite so bad for the *moment* as it might have been. . . . Better at present not mention the Leyland difficulty to *anyone.*" (L 1175-6) J. R. Parsons was a picture dealer.

Letter 53

1. CR 233.

Letter 55

1. Probably CR 233B, which belonged to Fanny Cornforth.

2. Retitled *The Roman Widow* (CR 236). To George Hake: "I believe now the subject [of *The Roman Widow*] is too 'painful' for the nerves of the British purchaser [Leyland]. However I shall paint it all the same." (L 1189)

3. Parts of this letter are quoted in Prinsep, "A Collector's Correspondence."

Letter 57

1. It was: however Rossetti had asked Leyland to pretend that the price was 900 guineas (see Letter 24).

2. Leyland evidently had said that he would be content if Rossetti dropped the Dante picture for other work. He had *not* said that he was still committed to the total purchase price of the Dante (2000 guineas).

3. The reason he couldn't "say when exactly" was that the face had been rucked in lining and Rossetti had had to start again on a fresh canvas (see Letter 73).

4. Probably CR 236A.

5. Rossetti preferred instead to talk the matter over with Brown and Howell—see L 1225-6.

Letter 59

1. Not entirely true. Rossetti had done most of the work on *Marigolds* (CR 235) the previous spring, but had held it in reserve to pay bills (see Letter 72).

Letter 61

1. A truncated version of this letter appears in L 1237.

Letter 63

1. Disingenuous, to say the least—he was hurriedly finishing the new canvas.

Letter 66

1. A different version of this letter, said to be a copy, appears in L 1250-1. Aside from differences in wording, punctuation, and paragraphing, the version in L adds a paragraph at the end which is not found in the original:

I have determined to satisfy myself with this picture, and have for that reason painted it three times, to say nothing of several other beginnings. Thus, if you hear at any time of two other *Proserpines de par le monde*, you must clearly understand that your own is the last in order of production and the first in merit.

An altered version of this paragraph is included in Letter 73.

Letter 67

1. The "particular reason" was that the version he had placed with Parsons had not yet been sold. It remained unsold, and was bought back by Rossetti in February.

Letter 71

1. Actually the 22nd.

Letter 72

1. The "money call" was Rossetti's desire to buy back the other *Proserpine* from Parsons. Leyland did not accept this offer, but Graham did, at a lower price (650 guineas, for a picture Rossetti considered "not a very important or laborious one").

2. Retitled *Marigolds*, CR 235.

Letter 73

1. This letter clarifies the confusion which seems to surround the history of this picture. Ms. Surtees catalogs eight versions of the painting, but there were only seven. The works listed by Ms. Surtees as R.5 and R.7 are one and the same, since R.5 was returned to Rossetti and then sent on to Leyland in lieu of the damaged R.6. Part of the confusion undoubtedly stems from Rossetti's mention of "seven

different canvases" (L 1253), but it will be noted that in the same letter to Brown he only describes six versions. (The seventh was executed much later, in 1881-1882.)

2. Leyland owned two early works by Alphonse Legros, *Le Maitre de Chapelle* and *The Rehearsal*.

Letter 74

1. Of his brother William Michael to Lucy Brown, on 31 March.

2. To Brown: "I am getting on with Leyland's picture, but feel bored and languid about it. . . . Leyland wrote proposing to come here 'for a few hours' last Sunday, but I put him off, the picture being not at the best juncture to show. I don't know if he'll be huffed." (L 1271)

3. CR 237, never executed in oil.

4. *The Shadow of Death*, being offered by Agnew for £11,000.

Letter 79

1. The "large Leighton" was *Syracusan Bride Leading Wild Beasts to the Temple of Diana*, and Leyland also sold two Turners, *Whale Ship* and *Queen Adelaide Disembarking at Southampton*.

2. *Ecce Ancilla Domini!*, CR 44, bought by Agnew from the estate of John Heugh for £388.10s., resold to Graham for £425.

Letter 80

1. Actually the painting had been seen by George Rae before it went up for auction, and he had purchased it for £126.

2. To Brown, 10 June: "If it proved necessary for me to ask Leyland to run down one day next week, could you come with him or meet him—going back with him or not just as you pleased. . . . a vis-à-vis with L. is a dreadful prospect." (L 1292) Brown evidently declined the honor, since Rossetti had to write again on 15 June: "Suppose you just trundle down here at once, and I would then write to Leyland to ask him, saying you were here. Thus you would be snugly ensconced out of the way of the joint journey." (L 1297)

Letter 81

1. Whistler's one-man show contained thirteen paintings and fifty etchings. To Brown, 31 May: "I think I twig the motive power. He must have finished the Leyland portraits, and persuaded L. that they were sure to be hung badly if sent to the R. A.—whereupon L., rather than see himself hoisted, paid bang out for an independent show of them. I have no doubt at this juncture it will send Whistler sky-high, and Leyland will probably buy no one else any more! I believe Leyland's picture will set the fashion in frills and buckles." (L 1287)

Letter 82

1. To Brown: "His big Leighton fetched—what do you think? £2,677! and the thing is really bad even of its own kind!" (L 1298)

Letter 85

1. CR 240.

2. The enlargement was undertaken, and the final size of the painting was 62 X 42. It was sold to Murray Marks in February at the price named.

Letter 86

1. Morris and Company.

2. Rossetti was designing wallpaper for Leyland.

3. George Wardle, chief designer for Morris and Company.

Letter 87

1. Leyland balked at the price of the *Astarte* (see Letters 88 and 89) and refused

both paintings. *Astarte Syriaca* (CR 249) was sold to Clarence Fry, and no new version of *Pandora* (CR 224) was begun until 1879, and then not on so grand a scale.

Letter 89

1. *A Sea–Spell* (CR 248), sold to Leyland for 800 guineas.
2. "Kubla Khan," 11. 37-41.
3. A truncated version of this letter appears in L 1345-6.

Letter 92

1. To Brown, 23 September: "I have somehow got through a new Leyland picture of the usual kind though in a very seedy state of health." (L 1354)
2. Graham's son had died from an accidental overdose of morphine.

Letter 101

1. *Veronica Veronese, Proserpine, The Roman Widow*, and *Lilith*, which Rossetti had been retouching (see L 1413-4).

Letter 102

1. CR 261, at first refused by Leyland, then commissioned by him as a *Hero* but never completed, finally sold to him as *Mnemosyne* in 1881.
2. Actually he had already sounded out Clarence Fry (L 1446) and been refused.

Letter 105

1. I. e. commissioned as a *Hero*.

Letter 106

1. The painting had begun as a version of the *Astarte Syriaca* commissioned by Clarence Fry, hence Leyland's use of this title.

Letter 107

1. Perhaps a reference to the demonstration of mesmerism which Rossetti had staged in the garden of Cheyne Walk, and to which Leyland had been invited (Pedrick, *Life with Rossetti*, p. 99).

Letter 108

1. Rossetti had succeeded in producing the required sonnet mentioned in Letter 107—"A Sea–Spell (for a picture)."

Letter 111

1. In 1877 Miss Adelaide Watt, the owner of Speke Hall, came of age, and she wished to take up residence. Leyland therefore moved his family to nearby Woolton Hall, built in 1704 by the Molyneux family and later redesigned by the distinguished neo-Classical architect Robert Adam.

Letter 112

1. Rossetti had just returned from three months at Hunter's Forestall, Herne Bay, where he had been recovering from an operation for hydrocele.

Letter 113

1. In 1878 Rossetti gave some thought to exhibiting but abandoned the idea—see John Nicoll, *The Pre–Raphaelites* (London: Studio Vista, 1970), p. 415.

Letter 114

1. Probably the former owner of Cartledge's Temperance Hotel, where Rossetti and Lizzie Siddal had stayed.

Letter 116

1. Leyland's eldest daughter, Mrs. Stevenson Hamilton, died in Italy at the age of twenty. On the occasion of her wedding the previous summer Rossetti described

her to Jane Morris as "so plain that with all her money she has had to marry a man twice her own age & with 3 kids ready made." (Quoted by Ms. Surtees, CR 346, n. 6)

Letter 118

1. *The Day Dream*, CR 259.

Letter 119

1. Probably the replica of the *Blessed Damozel* (CR 244.R.1) which occupied Rossetti for several years. Leyland finally purchased it in lieu of the *Hero* commission (see Letters 121 and 126).

2. Rossetti penciled some words on the margin of this letter which undoubtedly served as part of his reply: "I was glad to hear of the sale in the Times & will see the number. You will perceive how much worse my own forebodings were, since in my proposal to you I took off abt 120 per cent."

Letter 127

1. *The Salutation of Beatrice* (CR 260).

Letter 129

1. This proposed replica was never completed.

Letter 130

1. *Dante's Dream*, bought by the Corporation of Liverpool for 1500 guineas.

2. Unidentified.

Letter 134

1. The reference to Dunn is puzzling, since other evidence dates this letter as autumn 1881, yet Dunn had left Rossetti's employ the previous spring.

2. Leyland's friendship did raise an objection, namely that he did not like replicas of his pictures in circulation, so he bought up this replica as well.

Index

Adam, Robert, 106.
Agnew, Thomas and Sons, 64, 105.
Allingham, William, 100, 101.
Angeli, Helen Rossetti, ix, 100, 101.

Bader, Dr. Charles, 13.
Bibby, Messrs. and Sons, xii, 35.
Botticelli, Sandro, xiii.
Boyd, Alice, 101.
Brown, Ford Madox, xiii, xvii, xviii, 9, 18, 19, 65, 100, 102-106.
Brown, Lucy, 105.
Browning, Robert, xvi, xxii, xxiv, xxvi, xxviii.
Bryson, John, xi.
Buckley, Jerome, x.
Burne-Jones, Edward, xiii, xvii, 3, 16, 66, 101.

Cartledge, 83, 106.
Cattermole, John, xi.
Christie, Manson, and Wood, 9, 64, 65, 86.
Coleridge, S. T., 70.
Cooper, Robert, x.
Cornforth, Fanny, xi, xv, xxi, 103.
Cowper-Temple, Mrs. William, 82.
Crivelli, Carlo, xiii.

Doughty, Oswald, ix, x, xviii, xxxiii, 101.
Dunn, H. T., xi, xxi, xxii, xxvi, 55, 76, 91, 92, 102, 103, 107.
Dunlop, Walter, xxi, xxii, xxvii.

Fleming, G. H., x.
Ford and Dickinson, 9, 35, 45, 60, 80, 87, 90, 100.
Fredeman, William, x, xxxiv.
Fry, Clarence, 106.

Gainsborough, Thomas, 95.
Gee, Miss, 24, 25, 102.
Giorgione, xiii.
Gozzoli, Benozzo, 24.
Graham, William, x, xvii, xxi, xxiv, xxvii, 11, 16, 22, 23, 26, 27, 30, 36, 47, 50, 67, 72, 85, 100-106.
Gull, W. W., 13, 15, 101.

Hake, George, xi, xxii, 104.
Hamilton, Mrs. Stevenson, 84, 85, 106.
Hardy, Thomas, xxviii.
Harrison, Martin, x.
Heaton, Ellen, 101.
Herbert, J. R., 14, 101.
Heugh, John, xxi, xxii, xxvii, 64, 105.
Hilton, Timothy, x.
Hosman, R. S., x.
Howard, Ronnalie, x.
Howell, C. A., xvii, xxi, 6-8, 11, 13, 15, 18, 22, 35, 37, 39, 42, 47, 65, 71, 100, 101, 103, 104.
Hunt, Holman, xvi, xxii, 61.
Hunt, J. D., x.

Jameson, Frederick, 101.
Johnston, Robert, x.

109

110